S*U*UR MILK

& Other Saskatchewan crime stories.

Barb Pacholik
& Jana G. Pruden

2007

UNIVERSITY OF
REGINA

CANADIAN PLAINS
RESEARCH CENTER

The authors may be contacted via the publisher:
Canadian Plains Research Center
University of Regina
Regina, Saskatchewan S4S 0A2
Canada
Tel: (306) 585-4758/Fax: (306) 585-4699
e-mail: canadian.plains@uregina.ca/http://www.cprc.uregina.ca

Library and Archives Canada Cataloguing in Publication
Pacholik, Barb, 1965-
Sour milk and other Saskatchewan crime stories / Barb Pacholik
and Jana G. Pruden.

Includes bibliographical references.
ISBN 978-0-88977-197-0
1. Crime—Saskatchewan—History—20th century. 2. Criminals—
Saskatchewan—History—20th century. I. Pruden, Jana G., 1974- II.
University of Regina. Canadian Plains Research Center III. Title.
HV6809.S3P33 2007   364.1'0971240904   C2007-904324-0

Cover design: Duncan Campbell, Regina, Saskatchewan.
Printed and bound in Canada by Houghton Boston, Saskatoon

Publishers Note
We acknowledge the financial support of the Government of
Canada through the Book Publishing Industry Development
Program (BPDIP) for our publishing activities. We acknowledge the
support of the Canada Council for the Arts for our publishing
program.

The publisher would also like to thank Garrett Wilson (Regina),
Jenny MacDonald (Regina), Brett Matlock (Lumsden) and Jesse
Matlock (Lumsden), for having read the manuscript. Their
comments and insights were greatly appreciated.

Contents

Acknowledgments

We would very much like to thank our families and friends for their endless support and patience throughout this project.

We are also grateful to Nick Miliokas for his insights and direction, Vaughan McIntyre for his feedback, and proofreader Ian Hamilton for his corrections.

We are thankful to Regina lawyer Bill Johnson for fielding our questions; to Dr. Jeffrey Pfeifer at the University of Regina for sharing his research materials; and to the *Regina Leader-Post* and our colleagues for the support shown to us throughout the project.

We are indebted to court staff around the province for pulling piles of files and making us feel welcome while we hung around looking at them, and to the resources of the Saskatchewan and National Archives and the Regina Public Library's Prairie History Room.

We would also sincerely like to thank Brian Mlazgar and the Canadian Plains Research Center for giving us this fantastic opportunity. It has been more interesting and enlightening than we could possibly have imagined.

Finally, we would like to acknowledge the fine work of the reporters and writers who covered these cases before us. Without them, the facts and details of many Saskatchewan crime stories would have gone unrecorded, and would now be lost to time.

That, we believe, would have been a crime.

Authors' Note

To present these stories in a readable way, we have at times recreated scenarios based on court documents and transcripts, police evidence, news reports, pictures, and, in some cases, our own observations and notes.

That said, we've tried not to take liberties with thoughts or feelings, or make unreasonable inferences. Anything that appears in quotations is a direct quote as recounted by the people involved.

Unfortunately, people's recollections are not perfect—nor for that matter are historical records, court documents and news accounts. This was even more problematic for us in some of the historical criminal cases, where records of names, dates and other crucial details can vary wildly.

In these situations, or where separate accounts of a scenario conflict or differ completely, we've chosen what we considered to be the most likely version of events based on the material available.

The stories in this book are snapshots of a moment in crime. Some of the people we've written about may have done one terrible or foolish thing and gone on to live perfectly upstanding lives, never again gracing the inside of another police station, courtroom or jail cell. Others were—or are—incorrigible, destined to spend the rest of their lives behind bars.

It should be said that there are people in this book who maintain their innocence despite being convicted of a crime. In these cases, we have accepted the version of events that satisfied the judge or jury.

Where noted, we have used pseudonyms to comply with court-ordered publication bans. These pseudonyms are entirely fictitious, and any resemblance of these names, in whole or in part, to real life individuals is entirely coincidental.

Jana Pruden and Barb Pacholik
May 2007

"How many people's private lives would seem bizarre if they were absolutely exposed? Every person has an area of insanity in their lives."

— Robert Kieling

Grocery Misconduct

WHEN STUART NEUBAUER THOUGHT BACK ON IT, THERE WAS one thing he would change.

"I'd turn back the clock," he said. "And on the 20th of November I would have handed in my immediate resignation. I wouldn't have been there on the 21st."

But, despite any later regrets, Neubauer did not hand in his resignation on November 20. In fact, he never even thought about it.

Instead, he turned up for his night shift at the downtown Swift Current Safeway store on the evening of November 21, 1986 just as he always did: Early, eager and ready to work.

Neubauer got a part-time job at Swift Current's downtown Safeway store when he was 16, and liked it immediately. He devoted so much energy to his work at the store that his grades began to slip, and when he was offered full-time hours, he dropped out of high school and started working at Safeway full time.

From his first job bagging groceries, Neubauer had worked his way up within the company and, at 23, had a promising future in the grocery business. Most recently he'd been assigned to the freezer and dairy areas, where he stocked and ordered bread, frozen food and dairy products. It was a position he enjoyed, and he worked hard at it.

Living at home with his parents, Neubauer spent his free time reading financial magazines and the Bible and watching religious shows on satellite TV. He was a member of Jimmy Swaggart ministries and sponsored two foster children. A strapping man of 6'1" and more than 200 pounds, Neubauer was athletic and liked sports, especially martial arts, and had earned a green belt in karate. He spent six hours every morning poring over his investments, considering theories he'd read and working to apply them to the stock market.

On the evening of November 21, Stuart Neubauer showed up early for his overnight shift because an order of ice cream had come in and he didn't want it to melt.

The night was uneventful at first. Routine chores. Coffee at a new all-night restaurant with co-workers. A rattling pizza freezer in need of repair.

Neubauer asked the night manager, Kelly Kearns, to approve a couple of overtime hours so he could fix the freezer before the end of the shift. Kearns reluctantly approved the overtime, and Neubauer went to work on the broken machine. He punched out at 6:00 a.m., went home and lay awake for several hours.

Kelly Kearns never went home.

Inside a little house just across the street from the grocery store, Kearns' fiancée, Valerie Fitzpatrick, knew something was wrong. Kearns always came straight home after work or called if he was going to be late. He wasn't the type to go out without telling her. Worried, she called some of Kearns' co-workers and friends from the store, and a search was soon underway.

When Kearns still hadn't turned up a few hours later, everyone understood it was serious.

Neil Collier, a co-worker and good friend of Kearns, began collecting money to help pay for newspaper and TV ads to expand the search. Neubauer kicked in $10. As he pulled the money out of his wallet, he asked Collier whether there was anyone who would want Kearns killed.

"Stuart, I don't even want to think about that," Collier said, walking away in disgust.

It wasn't the first time Neubauer had caught his co-workers off guard. He was an outsider, and many of them found him odd and off-putting. He'd been seen meditating in the parking lot, and practising martial arts moves inside the store when he thought no one was around.

"I seen him once spinning a mop handle around, like you would see in karate movies," co-worker Tim Johnson said. "I've seen him kick the cooler door one time at my head level, and there were footprints on the door where he kicked it."

But no one at the store recalled any real trouble between Neubauer and Kearns. The two appeared to be neither friends nor enemies, just co-workers.

As Neubauer said, "The best way to describe it would be a casual working relationship. I knew him as Kelly Kearns."

That the two were not great friends was no surprise. In almost every way, they couldn't have been more different.

Where Neubauer was a loner, Kelly was a team player, a high school quarterback who still played football, hockey and baseball with passion. He was the union's shop steward and president of the local, widely known for going to the mat for his union and its members, once even vandalizing a truck during a volatile labour dispute.

But though Kearns could be short-tempered and verbally aggressive, he was also commanding and quick, and people liked him. At 27, he'd been rapidly climbing the ranks of the Safeway store, and despite some explosive earlier run-ins with store management, many there saw his potential.

"I was looking for a future store manager candidate to be moved out of Swift Current into stores throughout Saskatchewan," manager Chris Christie said. "Kelly had shown me great leadership qualities through the last five years."

It was those leadership qualities that lead Christie, in the fall of 1986, to promote Kearns to a management position, passing over another ambitious and equally qualified employee: Stuart Neubauer.

The day after Kearns disappeared, a police officer asked Neubauer to come to the police station for an interview. Neubauer arrived with a detailed chronology of his activities around the time the night manager went missing—including a couple of "oddities" he'd noticed that night, like a faint, odd smell in the grocery store. Neubauer also volunteered some opinions about his co-worker.

"Kelly isn't the angel that everybody thinks he is," he said.

From the conversation, the officer believed Neubauer wanted someone to search the store. Several officers did, but found nothing.

Days became weeks, and though the search had expanded throughout Western Canada, there was still no sign of Kelly Kearns.

When Kearns had been gone nearly a month and any leads had appeared to run dry, Christie offered Neubauer Kearns' job running the night crew. Neubauer accepted the promotion, and it was decided he would begin the position in January, after a three-week vacation. He was going to spend his time off at home in Swift Current; he said he wanted to be around when Kearns was found.

He was.

On January 12, fifty-two days after Kearns disappeared, a plumber working on a compressor in the bowels of the Safeway store was overcome by the smell of rotting meat. When he went to find the source of the smell, he saw an arm.

Kearns' body was found wrapped in garbage bags and trussed with wire from a store garbage baler. He was in a room of cooling and compressing equipment, lying beside a fan which vented outdoors.

Police arrested Neubauer that evening and charged him with murder.

Testifying at his own trial inside a packed Swift Current courtroom, Neubauer blamed it all on a large can of Emerald Isle fruit cocktail, which he said Kearns threw at him in a stockroom ambush during that ill-fated November shift. The large, heavy can rifled past his head, he said, so close it ruffled his hair when it passed.

Neubauer said he heard the can hit a set of steel doors, and turned to see Kearns posturing for a fight.

"I looked at him and he just looked back at me and said, 'What are you going to do about it?'" Neubauer testified. "He said, 'Come on, let's go for it.'"

Neubauer said Kearns called him names—wimp, stupid, idiot—and egged him on with obscenities and insults.

"All I could think was, 'Don't hit him, don't hit him. Just stay calm and this will pass,'" Neubauer said.

But it didn't pass. So Neubauer hit Kearns twice, first with an elbow to the temple, then a karate chop to the neck. It was over in seconds, Neubauer said, just bang, bang.

After the hits, Kearns' eyes rolled back and he collapsed. Like a rag doll, said Neubauer. Like a building falling to the ground.

"He was lying there," Neubauer testified. "And I just looked down at him and I said, 'Are you satisfied now?'"

There was no answer.

Kearns wasn't breathing and didn't have a pulse. Neubauer walked outside for a minute then came back, trussed up the body and took it to the compressor room. Then he unloaded some cottage cheese, filled the milk fridge and topped off the eggs. He told a co-worker Kearns had gone home early and left him with extra work to do.

"I didn't want to hit him," Neubauer cried in court. "It was just—it was just everything I could do to just not."

A simple and straightforward case of self-defence, that's what Neubauer's lawyers called it. Defence attorney

Murray Walter said Neubauer could easily have been killed himself if the can of fruit cocktail had hit its mark, and reacted instinctively to protect himself as he was being attacked.

Walter said Neubauer had suffered greatly before Kearns body was found.

"We can well imagine the agony that Stuart must have been going through," Walter told the jury. "The inner turmoil he must have been going through in this period of time."

Crown prosecutor Jack Hagemeister took a different view of the grocery manager's murder. To him, Neubauer's motive was simply "a secret, lingering, smouldering jealousy and hatred."

After a short deliberation, the jury returned its verdict: Guilty of second-degree murder. Neubauer was sentenced to life in prison, with no chance of parole for ten years.

"I did my work as diligently as possible and purposely never caused an innocent man, woman or child any problems with the unfortunate exception of Kelly's relatives," reads a "Last Will and Testimony," which police found charred and ripped, hidden inside Neubauer's bedroom after the murder. "But any man knows everybody has a point at which he will take no more."

A Good and Faithful Servant

JOHN MORRISON FELT LIKE A FAILURE.

Raising his axe over his head, the wiry hired man easily sliced through the scrub trees, clearing land he didn't own. It had been that way since he had come to Canada from Scotland as a boy. His mother dead and his father unable to care for him, Morrison had become a "home child," working for farm families filling the fledgling nation. He was far from being a child anymore, but home was currently the McArthur farm in the North-West Territories; Saskatchewan would not become a province for another five years.

Cutting away the brush for Alexander McArthur, Morrison thought about how hard he worked for his meagre wages—and how easily they were lost. He had squandered several hundred dollars. His depression and disgust with himself deepened.

Morrison remembered the letter he had sent back home a month ago. No one had bothered to reply.

He was only 27 years old, but Morrison had tired of his short life.

With each swing of his axe under the hot prairie sun, the quiet and moody Morrison refined his suicide plan. He thought of Maggie McArthur. Dear Maggie. Just 15 years old, and on the brink of becoming a woman.

Morrison would make her a woman–then he would take his life.

All that stood in his way was her father.

Alexander McArthur, Sandy as his friends called him, was everything that Morrison never would be. The 44-year-old contractor from Ontario had founded this town in 1882. Indeed, this was Arthur City until Ottawa decided otherwise, preferring "Welwyn" from its namesake in England. A prize-winning stock breeder, member of town council, school board official, and the postmaster, McArthur commanded respect.

By contrast, Morrison was, as the Moosomin newspaper would later describe him, a "good and faithful servant." He had worked on and off for the McArthur family for the last eight years. Morrison had no quarrel with his employer. But now his boss stood between him and Maggie.

Alexander McArthur would have to die.

A few days later, Morrison brought his axe back to the house, to sharpen it. He was having second thoughts after playing with the McArthur children. He joined football practice that evening with his friends at a neighbouring farm. Morrison lingered, chatting with his buddies. It had begun to rain, and he hoped it might rain all night so he would not have to return home to carry out his plan. But the skies cleared. He ran the four miles back to the McArthur homestead.

Wet with rain and sweat, Morrison slipped off his boots, picked up his axe and walked through the kitchen. A lamp was still burning on the table. Maggie had left the lamp lit every night since her baby brother was born two weeks earlier. Morrison strode upstairs to the bedroom he shared with 11-year-old Dempsey. Morrison took his revolver from out of his trunk so he could shoot himself if McArthur awoke.

It was just after midnight on June 9, 1900, when

Morrison quietly walked back down the stairs to the master bedroom, off the kitchen. In the dim light, he could see McArthur sound asleep. "Will I put out the light?" Morrison asked, wanting to be certain no one was awake. There was silence. Just as he had done with the brush earlier that day, the faithful servant raised his axe above his 5'6" frame—and brought it down on his master's head.

Across the room in another bed, McArthur's 40-year-old wife awoke and sat up. Morrison had always liked Sarah. She was like a mother to him.

But now he used his axe to slice into her head.

As Sarah lay dying, it occurred to Morrison she might want her children with her in the afterlife. His blows found the newborn, lying next to his mother, and 6-year-old Mamie, asleep at the foot of her mother's bed. Using the flat of his axe, Morrison struck out at Henry, the 2-year-old asleep in a cradle between his parents. Although injured, the three youngest McArthurs would survive; 4-year-old brother Russell, asleep with his father, would not.

Covered in McArthur blood, Morrison climbed the stairs and went first to Dempsey. He caught the boy across the back of the head with such force that the axe left two marks in the plaster ceiling.

Morrison went to the front bedroom, above the post office, where Maggie and Charlie slept. He lifted the 8-year-old boy from his bed. Maggie heard her brother's cries in the darkness, the blows of the axe, then his moaning. Neighbours found the child's lifeless body lying face down on the floor in a pool of blood spilled from his head. The axe had sliced through the floor boards.

There was no one to stand in Morrison's way. Maggie was his.

Sitting on her bed, he said nothing as he worked at his revolver. He rose and put the gun on the table, took off his pants, and climbed into Maggie's bed. He loved her deeply, the killer said. He even loved the ground on which she walked. Of course, she didn't know that. He wondered why she had been so cool towards him the last few days. Her father out of the way, Morrison could have the girl. He did try—but a struggling Maggie resisted his advances and her would-be lover failed in his attempts.

Then he pointed his revolver at Maggie's head. It misfired, leaving her unscathed.

Morrison turned the gun on himself to complete his suicidal plan. He pulled the trigger. Nothing happened.

The hired man put on his clothes and walked back down the stairs, past the carnage, and out to the barn with McArthur's double-barrelled shotgun and the axe in tow.

Maggie heard a shot ten minutes later and left her bedroom. She re-lit the lamp to discover the maimed bodies of her family. It was a half-mile through darkness to the Jamieson farm.

Albert Hughes, who had played football with Morrison just a few hours earlier, cautiously approached his friend. He lay wounded in one of the stable stalls. Morrison had put a stick through the triggers on the double-barrelled shotgun before lifting the muzzle to his heart. When he pushed on the stick with his foot, only one barrel fired. Morrison was still alive, but with a gaping wound in his side. He tried to finish the job with his handgun, but it would not fire. He had failed again.

Hughes asked for an explanation. Morrison told him how he wanted to end his life. "I thought I would take them all with me," he said.

The man who wanted to die was nursed back to health, while McArthur, his wife and their sons slaughtered in their beds were laid to rest in a single, 12 x 6.5 foot grave in Moosomin's cemetery. As each of the five coffins was lowered, Maggie, the only one to escape physically unscathed, collapsed, sobbing next to her uncle.

It's a long way from Welwyn to Regina, but Amos Kinsey didn't mind. He had been one of the first to find the McArthurs. Now he wanted to see their killer die.

The morning air was cool and crisp on January 17, 1901 as Morrison climbed the same scaffold in Regina where Louis Riel had been hanged fourteen years earlier. The noose was already around Morrison's neck when he interrupted his executioner.

"I would like to say something for the good of the world," Morrison said. "Life, at best, is very short, and I hope that what I have done will be a warning to others to live that short life in a different way to what I have done." The young man added, "Life, I say, is short and the sword is always hanging over us, and we do not know how soon it will drop."

Captain Gillam of the Salvation Army recited the Lord's Prayer. At the words "deliver us from evil," the hangman drew back the bolt on the scaffold. The trap door did not fail.

Room 104

HE WAS LARGER THAN LIFE, THE KIND OF PERSON YOU EITHER loved or hated. That's what people in Swift Current said about Ed Lang.

But love him or hate him, no one could deny that Ed Lang was a powerful man.

At 72, Lang was a successful rancher, well-known in his community and a fixture in the Canadian cattle industry. He was considered by some to be one of the most success- ful cattlemen in the province, maybe the country.

On a fall day in 2000, Lang called Emily Bobryk, a woman he'd been seeing on and off for a few years. He reached her at her mother's house, and told her he want- ed to see her. Arriving at Bobryk's house in Regina, Lang helped her pick out a few outfits, then drove her to Swift Current, where he lived. Bobryk fell asleep on the drive, and woke up outside The Rodeway Inn, a motel on the edge of town.

The two went into the office and checked in. Lang told Bobryk to use a fake name, so she signed in as 'June Bobryk,' using her middle name instead of her actual first name. The pair rented a couple of rooms, which Lang paid for with his gold card. Bobryk took Room 104, and Lang left her there alone for the night.

The next morning, Ed Lang came back to the Rodeway Inn with his 36-year-old son Doug and another man, and the three men began working busily in Room 105, drilling holes in the wall and hooking up a VCR and TV.

In Bobryk's room next door, the men set up a clock-radio camera they had rented from a local spy shop and pointed it at the bed. Then they attached a tiny microphone under the desk. Emily wanted to see how it worked, so she pushed Lang's son, Doug, onto the bed and laid down next to him, both of them laughing and goofing around for the camera.

THE PHONE AT DICKSON AGENCIES rang the morning of September 29. Dorothy Gatzke reached to answer it.

"Good morning, Dickson Agencies," she said.

"Hi," said the woman on the other end. "Is Paul Elder there? I'm with '*Maclean*' magazine and I'm doing an interview on a different sort of people."

Gatzke told the woman her boss at the insurance agency—and Swift Current's mayor—wasn't in.

When Elder got back to the office a short time later, Gatzke passed along the message.

"But she didn't sound like a reporter," Gatzke warned. "She was vague and hesitant. She was faltering, like she didn't know what to say next."

After returning the call, Mayor Elder agreed.

The woman was strange. She had asked to meet him at a motel, rather than his office at City Hall or at the insurance agency, saying she didn't have access to a car. And she didn't talk like a professional reporter.

"She sounded like she might be intoxicated," Elder observed.

Elder and Gatzke told city clerk Dianne Hahn about the phone call when she stopped by Dickson Agencies to renew her licence plates. Hahn was immediately suspicious. She called *Maclean's* and found out there were no reporters in the area working on stories for the national news magazine. Then Elder called the police.

Elder and Hahn pulled up to the Rodeway Inn just before 2:00 p.m., when the interview was to take place, and met a plainclothes officer in the parking lot. They walked together to Room 104, and knocked on the door.

On the other side, Emily Bobryk panicked.

She had been ready—equipped with two condoms, some vodka, and a plan to get Elder into bed—but seeing three people outside the door, she knew the afternoon would not go as planned.

Staying as quiet as she could, Bobryk grabbed the clock radio and microphone and threw them in with the other stuff she'd brought. Next door, the Langs scrambled to clean up their room, too, stuffing everything into a bag and taking off.

Bobryk got drunk that evening, and Lang drove her back to Regina in his white pickup truck. He gave her $400 of the $5,000 he had promised her.

"I'll get the fucker yet," she remembered him saying.

The next time Bobryk and Lang spoke, it was she who called him.

"I'm coming down for a good fucking time this week-end so have your briefcase ready and have a lot of fucking coin in your pocket," she said. "It's going to cost you."

And it did. Bobryk was working for the RCMP.

Ever since the motel meeting, police in Swift Current had been investigating whether the Langs had tried to blackmail Elder in an attempt to hurt his bid for re-election. The investigators had convinced Bobryk to help them. She was wearing a wire when she talked to Lang at another Swift Current motel.

"I think he's smarter than I thought he was," Lang told Bobryk, while the tape was rolling.

The same could not be said for Ed and Doug Lang.

They were charged with conspiracy to commit extortion and attempted extortion for the scheme. When Ed Lang was arrested, police seized several items from his vehicle, including a receipt for a one-week video camera rental and a "Don Robinson for Mayor" election poster.

Testifying in their own defence in a Swift Current court, the father and son admitted they attempted to lure the mayor into a tryst, but said they never intended to record it.

They were only hoping to satisfy their own curiosity, they said, not blackmail the mayor.

"I wasn't going to use no photos or tapes," Ed Lang told a packed Swift Current courtroom.

Certainly, the elder Lang had no love for Mayor Elder. Elder had once shut down a feedlot proposal in which Lang had invested several hundred thousand dollars, leaving Lang holding a costly property he couldn't unload.

Elder was chasing businesses out of town, Lang said. Furthermore, he suspected Elder of smoking marijuana and womanizing.

"I thought he was leading a double life," Lang told court. "He was portraying a holier-than-thou image and I heard rumours to the other."

At the start of the trial, the Langs' lawyer, Aaron Fox, promised the jury: "This was probably one of the most hare-brained, stupid schemes you've ever heard of."

Still, stupid isn't the same as guilty. After seven hours of deliberation, a seven-woman, five-man jury declared the Langs not guilty of either charge.

While the Langs survived the trial more or less unscathed, it took its toll on Elder.

In the months that followed, he had to sell his insurance business, his marriage broke up and he had a heart attack.

A year later, Elder attempted to win a fourth term as mayor. He was defeated.

The Long Ride

IT WAS THE BRAKE LIGHT THAT CAUGHT HIS EYE. SHINING brilliant red in the darkened parking lot, not too long after a snowy Sunday night became a frigid Monday morning.

It didn't sit right with Sergeant John Lyon—Al, as his friends called him—and thirteen years as a cop had given him a pretty good gut instinct. So Lyon pulled his cruiser into the lot to check it out.

The car was a blue Beaumont with Saskatchewan plates. A nice two-door '66, just a couple of years old.

Through the frost-covered windows, Lyon could see there was someone inside, and as he approached the passenger-side door, a man jumped out at him. The guy was heavy-set, with a day's worth of stubble on his chin and close-cut red hair receding above nervous eyes.

He stuck a gun in Lyon's stomach. "The gun is fully loaded," he said. "I'll shoot if you make one move."

The man took Lyon's service revolver, and handcuffed the officer with Lyon's own police-issue handcuffs. He seemed unsure of what to do next.

"I'm in very serious trouble," he told Lyon. "I have nothing to lose at this point."

When Lyon walked up the man had been trying to steal

the car, but couldn't get it going. Still unable to get the car started, he stuck the gun into Lyon's back and walked him toward a nearby apartment block hoping to commandeer another car—and another hostage. Lyon convinced him to take the police car instead.

As they walked through the lot, another police car approached.

"He's got an automatic to my back," Lyon told the two officers. "Don't try anything funny. Just go away."

The officers complied.

The man got into the driver's seat of Lyon's cruiser with Lyon at his side. With one hand on the steering wheel, the other pointing the gun at Lyon, he steered them out of town on the icy highway and into the cold winter night.

IN SOME WAYS, DAVID THURSTON BROWN had been running all his life.

His mother died before he turned 1, leaving him in the hands of his father, a drunk, and a mean one at that. It took Brown three years to complete Grade 3, and by Grade 9 he was done with school altogether. When he met Lyon, Brown was not yet 40, but had already spent more than half of his life in jail. His rap sheet included convictions for break and enter, theft, armed robbery, and burglary. He'd been sentenced in courtrooms in Melville, Regina, Calgary, Vancouver, Ottawa, Toronto and Montana. On that December day he was on parole for an armed robbery out of Manitoba, and terrified of going back to prison.

Brown had spoken the truth to Lyon: He had nothing to lose.

Ten minutes out of Regina, Brown uncuffed Lyon, and told him to take control of the cruiser. Brown moved to the back seat, pressing the cold metal muzzle of the gun against the back of Lyon's neck.

With police cars in hot pursuit, Brown grabbed the radio and growled at the dispatcher: "Get the monkeys off my tail or I'll shoot."

The cars behind them slowed and dropped into the distance.

Things were calm for a while, but Brown became agitated when he saw a locked gate pulled across the road at the Regway border crossing. There were two cars parked across the road just past it. Brown ordered Lyon to keep driving.

"Ram it and run the roadblock or I'll blow your head off," he said.

Lyon did as he was told.

THE CALL CAME IN TO THE sheriff's office in Scobey, Montana at 2:40 a.m.

Norman Fossen, who was manning the radios, immediately called the sheriff and two other officers, and the men scrambled out of bed and into action, driving a few miles north of town and making a roadblock with their cars. There were now more than thirty police officers, American and Canadian, closing in on Brown and his hostage from all sides.

Seeing the blockade outside Scobey, Brown told Lyon to stop in the middle of the highway. They were surrounded, and Brown held Lyon at gunpoint as they climbed out of the car.

The gun in Brown's hand went off.

There was a crack, a puff of smoke. The bullet whizzed by Lyon's chest and into the darkness.

Someone yelled to back off, and Brown pulled Lyon back into the car. The officers moved backed fast to give Brown more room.

Montana Sheriff Lyle Medders took the police radio, urging Brown to give himself up before he got into more trouble. Brown said he'd kill Lyon if the roadblock wasn't opened.

But Medders would not negotiate. He told Brown the road would not be opened under any circumstance. Brown asked for ten minutes to think it over.

After talking to Lyon inside the car for several minutes, Brown agreed to surrender.

The men came out of the car together with their hands in the air. Lyon had promised Brown he wouldn't be abused by the authorities in any way. He gave his word.

Three hours after it began, it was finished. Brown was held in a Plentywood jail and Lyon went back to Regina, where his wife and three children were waiting anxiously.

Before he left, he talked to a newspaper reporter in Scobey.

"It's frightening, there's no two ways about it," he said. "This is something any police officer can come up against, but you always think it will be somebody else."

Brown pleaded guilty to kidnapping, robbery with violence, and attempted auto theft. Sentencing Brown to sixteen years in prison, Judge E.L. Elliott said Brown was past rehabilitation, "a menace to the public at large."

"It is not at all possible to extend any sympathy to Brown," he said.

Lyon may not have felt the same way. He said the two had talked while on the road together, and maintained Brown had generally treated him well during the ordeal. What they talked about in the car that dark December morning remained between them.

LYON DIED IN 2005, AT THE AGE OF 70.

A scrapbook he kept tells the story of his meeting with Brown.

The newspaper clippings are yellowed and faded, with old tape rising from the pages. There are big front-page stories with bold headlines: "Policeman kidnapped; helps arrest suspect" and shorter ones; "Brown admits kidnapping."

There are stories about Brown's brief escape from the Regina Correctional Centre and a parolee information bulletin sent out by Toronto police just before Brown's release from prison in the summer of 1983. There are copies of police reports about the kidnapping, and photos taken at the Plentywood jail after Brown's arrest.

Tucked into the scrapbook is a crumpled white envelope containing a tarnished shell casing.

It's from the bullet that was shot from Sergeant Lyon's own Smith & Wesson .38 Special, his service revolver.

The bullet that whizzed by Lyon on the road near Scobey, Montana, but didn't hit him.

The one that could have changed everything.

Dreams and Nightmares

DAVID STOOD ON THE EDGE OF A GRAVEL ROAD JUST OUTSIDE the city of Saskatoon and watched two police officers walking through a field in the fading evening light. When the policemen reached a clump of bushes, they stopped.

"Yeah," one of the officers said finally, shouting back toward the road. "They're here."

David Thrienen went pale and began to shake.

"Up until now I thought it was a dream," he said, speaking to no one in particular.

SASKATOON'S NIGHTMARE BEGAN ON Father's Day, 1975, the day Dahrlyne Cranfield and Robert Grubesic set out together on their bicycles, off to explore the trails along the South Saskatchewan River.

Dahrlyne was 12, Robert 9. It was cool that morning, and Robert wore his light blue jacket with the eagle on it. He carried a little green toy airplane in one pocket, and a small comic book.

Their bicycles were found locked together later, the wheel on the smaller bike twisted and unrideable, but the children had vanished. Police searching the area found no other clues, and believed the children might have fallen into the river. It appeared to be a drowning. A terrible and tragic accident.

When two more children disappeared, it became something much, much worse.

It was six weeks later, the end of July. This time it was 8-year-old Samantha Turner and her best friend Cathy Scott, who was 7. The girls left their home in Sutherland for some ice cream and never came home.

After calling the police, the girls' families and residents of the close-knit community searched frantically throughout the night. Volunteers continued to comb the area for days afterward, working determinedly alongside police dogs and trained search teams looking for any trace of the two little girls.

This time the police knew it was not an accident. The public knew it, too, and fear gripped the city. Families kept their doors locked, parents refused to let their children out of the house despite the stifling heat of the prairie summer, and everyone regarded strangers with suspicion.

As hundreds of citizens continued to search for the children, dozens of police officers looked for the person who had taken them. Pulled off other investigations, the officers worked around the clock, poring over boxes of files sent to them by police forces around the country.

A pair of plainclothes police officers found David Thrienen changing a tire at a service station on August 12, three weeks after Samantha and Cathy disappeared. He was a tall, slim man in his late 20s, with dirty blonde hair and a pock-marked face. The officers watched him work for a bit before one of them approached. Thrienen and the officer chatted for a while, discussing tires, mostly, nothing serious.

The officers trailed Thrienen back to the city before approaching him again. This time they told him they were police officers, and asked him to come to the police station with them.

The officers didn't tell him why, and he didn't ask.

Thrienen's criminal record dated back more than a

decade to 1963, when he assaulted two 10-year-old girls in a movie theatre, and he'd been charged with indecent assault for another attack in 1973.

Most disturbingly to investigators, Thrienen had also been charged with killing a 16-year-old girl named Angela Huemer in Lethbridge, but escaped conviction because of critical holes in the evidence.

During the Lethbridge investigation, Thrienen told police he didn't remember anything about the night of the girl's death, just that he found himself out in the country with a body in the backseat and a feeling that he couldn't take it anymore.

Sitting in a cramped interrogation room with Saskatoon police detective Rusty Chartier, Thrienen swore he hadn't taken the children.

"Rusty, honest," he pleaded. "I had nothing to do with it."

Chartier didn't believe him. Neither did Gordon Twist.

Even before walking into the interrogation room, Corporal Twist knew in his gut that Thrienen was the guy. He tried another approach.

"You need help and you must help yourself before anybody can help you," he told Thrienen. "I can see by your eyes you want to tell me or somebody about those four children."

Thrienen asked to see a doctor, and when Twist promised he could, Thrienen's confession came gushing out.

"I killed them," he said. "I'll take you out to the bodies."

Dahrlyne and Robert were in a cluster of bushes just outside the city, Cathy and Samantha in a field northeast of Sutherland. Even the most seasoned police investigators were shocked and horrified by the gruesome scenes.

"I don't think we should elaborate on what we found or what we saw at all," Saskatoon Police Chief James Kettles said the next day. "This has to be the most horrendous, vicious thing I've seen in my time."

In the days that followed Thrienen gave several statements to police. With a cigarette burning almost constantly, he told them everything.

Thrienen said he spent Father's Day sitting on a park bench across from the Bessborough Hotel, thinking about his estranged wife and children in Alberta, and wondering where they were that day. It was there he met two children. Thrienen said the boy's bike was broken, and he asked them if they wanted ice cream. They did, so the girl locked up their bikes, and Thrienen took their hands and walked them to his car. He didn't stop for ice cream. Instead, he drove straight out of the city a few miles and pulled off the highway. Leaving Robert alone in the car, he took Dahrlyne into the bush, kissed her, then strangled her with her own jeans. He went back for Robert, taking the little boy by the hand to meet the same tragic fate. After Robert was dead, Thrienen drove home and went to bed early.

He found Cathy and Samantha in Sutherland after visiting his parents in Humboldt on a day off from work. Again, he lured the children to him with the promise of ice cream. It was easy, he said. He didn't even have to get out of the car.

The girls were quiet as he drove them away from the ice cream parlour.

"Nobody said nothing," Thrienen told the police. "They didn't cry. They sat at the back eating some candy or something."

He pulled off into a field, took the children out of the car and strangled them one by one. Then he drove home, picked up his gear and went fishing.

Describing the ghastly scenes to police, Thrienen seemed as surprised by his actions as everybody else.

"I just seem to turn into someone else," he told one officer. "Just wasn't myself. I don't know what it was. The next morning when I woke up it was just like a dream, a bad dream. It didn't even really bother me because I figured it was just a dream."

There were other children, too. Thrienen told the police he had once pulled a 10-year-old Saskatoon girl into his car and strangled her with a scarf. He dumped her unconscious body in a snow-covered field, and a farmer later found her wandering the land in a disoriented state. He also admitted luring a brother and sister into his car earlier that spring, but said the girl ran away and he let the boy go.

"Just one minute I'm me and the next minute I was someone else...," he said. "It's just like Dr. Jekyll and Mr. Hyde. One minute you're one person, the next minute you're a totally different person altogether."

Thrienen couldn't explain why he killed the children.

"I haven't got a clue," he said. "It started off innocent enough and ended up in tragedy. I think that's how you say it, anyways."

On the day his trial was supposed to begin in February 1976, Thrienen pleaded guilty to four counts of murder.

"We submit the accused is the most dangerous individual the city has ever seen," Crown prosecutor Wilf Tucker said. "In fact the most dangerous the province has ever seen."

Justice Ted Hughes agreed, and sentenced Thrienen to four consecutive life sentences with no chance of parole without government approval. Hughes vowed to personally write letters recommending Thrienen never be released from prison.

"A life under surveillance must be yours until death...," he said. "The fact is, no one's child, grandchild or great-grandchild must ever be subject to your presence in their midst."

Appearing before a parole board twenty-five years later, Thrienen agreed, and asked the board not to release him.

"I will spend the rest of my life in prison," he said. "I will die here. I'm where I belong."

Gold Watches and White Collars

WITH A FEW BUCKS IN HIS POCKET AND A CHEQUE IN HAND, Nick Bonamy left prison to begin life anew. He rode the bus from Prince Albert to Saskatoon and found an affordable hotel room before he went looking for a bank to cash his cheque. His only identification was a parole release card. The banks were not vying for his business. Bonamy explained his predicament to a sympathetic assistant branch manager at a credit union and, with some help from his parole officer, opened an account. He deposited most of his cheque, his earnings as a prison inmate.

Within weeks of his release on October 6, 2000, the ambitious parolee enrolled at the University of Saskatchewan as a mature student. "I'm a 52-year-old individual recently released from the penitentiary after serving 10 years of a life sentence," Bonamy wrote on his application. He registered for correspondence courses in computers, geography and geology. He was going to earn an undergraduate degree in computer science. Bonamy was eager to make a new start.

JIM MADDIN, THE MAYOR OF Saskatoon, was clearly excited as he stood poised to help cut the ribbon on the world's first GenoCentre. "A lot of good things are going to flow from this," he predicted. The Saskatoon GenoCentre was just the beginning of an ambitious plan to open 500 genetic testing clinics worldwide. Soon anyone just about anywhere would be able to buy (only $1,500 at the Saskatoon centre) their own geno passport, a personal genetic profile that would let clients know if they were at risk for an array of hereditary diseases.

At the nucleus of GenoCentre was its parent company Genometrics Corporation. Genetic data collected from GenoCentres around the world would flow to the Saskatoon headquarters. Located in Innovation Place, Genometrics fit well with the city's growing high tech industry. In fact, it was the nearby Canadian Light Source Synchrotron facility that had first attracted Dr. Nicolas Grimaldi, Genometrics' founder, to Saskatoon a year earlier. The biochemist and industrious entrepreneur recognized the city's potential.

Dr. Grimaldi had been at the helm of Vancouver-based Nicolas Grimaldi and Associates, a group of bioinformatics consultants, for the last fourteen years. A graduate of the University of Geneva, Grimaldi had designed software for the Sanger Institute, a renowned genome research centre in England. Reputed to have an IQ of 186, Grimaldi's intelligence and passion for science was—well—in his genes. He was a relative of the famous geneticist and Nobel laureate Paul Berg of Stanford University. Grimaldi had recently completed his work developing quality control software for the world-famous Human Genome Project and had been looking for a new opportunity.

The bilingual scientist met Genometrics' first investor while attending a social function at the Francophone Federation of Saskatchewan soon after his arrival in Saskatoon. The federation's president not only put money into the company, but was so taken with its founder, she recommended Grimaldi for the vacant treasurer's job. At the same November 15, 2000, meeting when Grimaldi was elected to the board, discussion turned to hiring a consultant to examine the feasibility of building a cultural centre in Saskatoon. Grimaldi knew someone who would be perfect for the job. His friend, a Vancouver urban development consultant for Management Technologies Incorporated, was paid $5,000 in advance and the remaining $11,050 in January 2001 after completing the report.

From his fine clothes to his expensive gold watch, the charismatic, articulate Grimaldi had an air of success about him. Originally from Monte Carlo, he was a cousin of Monaco's reigning royal family and was raised in Geneva as the son of a diplomat. For Genometrics' investors, even more impressive than Grimaldi himself was his creation—PhenGen. The copyrighted computer database of phenotopic and genotopic correlations could be invaluable for genetic studies. The business plan for the registered corporation also touted Genometrics 2000, data-mining software created by Grimaldi for the Human Genome Project. It all meant Genometrics Corporation could market individual mapping of a person's genome in a quick, cost-effective manner.

Members of the business, scientific, and medical communities applauded the GenoCentre at its grand opening on October 4, 2001. It was a great day for Genometrics' president and founder. He had come a long way in a year.

Perhaps surprisingly, Grimaldi didn't appear in any of the photographs taken at the opening.

DESPITE THE THREE CLASSES IN which he had enrolled, Nick Bonamy was no closer to getting a degree a year after his arrival in Saskatoon. He had not completed any of the assignments, or written a single exam. His parole officer received a call in November 2001 from the manager of the credit union where the parolee had opened his account. The manager had noticed a lot of money was moving in and out of Bonamy's personal account, as well as a business account for Management Technologies. Bonamy had opened it one day after the second cheque from the Francophone Federation had been authorized for the feasibility study he had co-authored with "André Lesperance," a fictitious character of his creation. Curiously, many of the funds transferred into the Management Technologies' account came from Nicolas Grimaldi. When Bonamy showed up to meet his parole officer on November 29, 2001, police were waiting.

The next day, Grimaldi was supposed to meet with computer giants IBM and Compaq to discuss multi-million-dollar deals. The meetings did not take place. With the arrest of Bonamy, also known as the smooth-talking Grimaldi—and by more than a dozen other aliases—Genometrics declared bankruptcy, and its sixteen employees were out of work. Bonamy's victims lost $313,000, including five investors who had put $150,000 into Genometrics. For one former employee and investor, "it instilled in me a diminished trust in humanity."

Bonamy saw things differently. "My life was shattered," the self-confident, self-centred cheat grumbled in a courtroom after his arrest. He was motivated by altruism, not greed, he said. "Everything that I had built in the past thirteen months was down the drain."

From almost the moment he walked out of prison, the phoney biochemist had begun synthesizing stories. He even lied to the university about what he had been doing in prison. It wasn't a life sentence. Perhaps it felt that way to the aging con, who had indeed served a good portion of his life behind bars. His criminal record began in 1972, when he diverted money to the terrorist group *Front de liberation du Québec* while working for that province's government. Over the next twenty-six years, he amassed sixty convictions in three different provinces. All but six were for theft or fraud.

When he left prison in October 2000, Bonamy had been paroled midway into a nine-year prison sentence for theft, fraud, and breach of copyright convictions. Working as a "computer programmer" in the mid 1990s, he had taken an Alberta community college for $900,000. He used the stolen money to subsidize a chain of paint and wallpaper stores in British Columbia. At the same time, the persuasive schemer sold pirated software to BC businesses. Still, the parole board was optimistic about Bonamy finally going straight. "It is encouraging that you have decided to make an effort to start your life over and face the future with a new degree of honesty," it said.

Bonamy was reborn as Dr. Grimaldi, and his deceit was as twisted as the DNA strands he claimed to study. His life story—birthplace, education, occupation, relatives—was all a lie. He forged a signature to get $9,350 in student loans for university classes he would never attend—money he could have used since he had no degree. His friend at Management Technologies was none other than Nick Bonamy, his alter ego. When police searched his home, they found a business plan from a Web site called sellthefarm.com. He had used the model to create the prospectus for Genometrics, founded less than two months after he left prison. What police did not find was the non-existent, supposedly valuable computer software programs that had enticed the investors.

In less than a year, Bonamy/Grimaldi had opened seven bank accounts. He had secured a $50,000 bank loan a month before the GenoCentre opened. The high-flying businessman e-mailed a Genometrics balance sheet to the account manager and wrote: "I will be in Vancouver tomorrow and Thursday to negotiate an agreement with the BC Cancer Institute and UBC Hospital. More info upon my return." The loan application was supported by tax returns, balance sheets and account statements that showed his income from Nicolas Grimaldi and Associates at $126,000 and his personal net worth at $849,000.

"Since the above listed material, especially the income tax returns, falls under the privacy act, I trust that you will ensure that the material remains within the Royal Bank's knowledge," read Bonamy's letter accompanying the documents. At the same time, he began floating NSF cheques between his accounts to artificially inflate his bank balance and secure further funds. The bank lost nearly $142,000.

Bonamy did not lie about one thing. He was in fact a researcher. The sharp imposter had a lot of time to study the world of genetics, computer software and business before he left prison. Among those taken in by the brilliant con was the president of one of the world's largest uranium mining companies; a former chemist from the National Research Council; and a respected medical doctor.

An unrepentant Bonamy pleaded guilty to four fraud-related charges and received a four-year prison sentence in addition to approximately a year he had already served. "My values might be different than other people's," he told his sentencing hearing nearly five years after the collapse of Genometrics. "I don't think twice about forging documents or uttering documents or lying if my purpose in doing so has a larger value than what I consider my credibility or my truthfulness." Throughout his criminal career, Bonamy has maintained the ends justified the means. As he saw it, Genometrics would save lives, and Grimaldi was merely his public name, no different than Mark Twain, Tennessee Williams or Frank Sinatra.

Over the years, he has had a lot of public names: Nicholas Kbonamy, Edouard Yvon Elzear Bonamie or Bonami, Nicholas or Nicolas Yvon Bonamy or Banamy, Yvon Edouard Bonami or Bonamie, Nicholas Yvon, Nicholas J. Bonamy, Nicholas Juppe Bomamy, Jos Edward Robert Richard, Nicolas or Nicholas Grimaldi, Nick Bunamy, and Nicolas Ives. He has given his birthplace as Romania, Switzerland, Monaco and Montreal. He has been married once, or maybe twice, and has had three different mothers and two fathers. His employment history is equally ambiguous.

A psychologist who examined him in prison might have come closest to the truth. His report notes that Bonamy—if that is really his name—feeds on stimulation, especially anti-social thrills, frauds and cons. It is entrenched in his genetic make-up.

Spotless to the End

CROUCHING BEHIND A PARKED CAR, THE 5'1" RUSSIAN WAR veteran looked even smaller as he waited across from the imposing Saskatchewan Legislative Building. Without gloves, his rough, stained hands felt the sting of the cold December air. It was three days after Christmas, and daylight was fast turning to dusk.

Valentine Schmidt still had an hour to wait. Time to think.

He had come to this country twelve years earlier in 1914—just two years after the newly constructed home for Saskatchewan's government saw its first legislative sparring. Back then, Valentine and his wife Rosie were also building a new life in this province. Valentine had apprenticed under his father as a blacksmith in their Russian homeland near the Black Sea. Those skills easily transferred to the Prairies, where Valentine worked in farming towns, such as Davin, Kendal and Sintaluta. In his work hammering and shaping metal, Valentine gained a reputation as a first-class tradesman. Inside his home, he also hit hard. His wife knew him for his iron fist.

Like her husband, Rosie's well-worn hands betrayed her status as a labourer. But while his were blackened by hot, dirty steel, hers tended to be scrubbed and scoured.

Up early in the morning, the mother of two put in long hours in other people's homes, washing laundry and polishing floors. That was her day job. She spent three hours each evening dusting and cleaning offices. Often, she did not return home until ten at night or later.

Rosie worked tirelessly and saved her money; Valentine worked sporadically and spent Rosie's meagre pay. The couple had left the countryside and bought a house in Regina in the early 1920s so Rosie could be closer to her sister. But in the city, Valentine struggled to find work and keep it. He often left in the spring and drifted to various jobs. He returned to his family in the fall and expected Rosie to support him.

He eventually went to work in the United States. Once settled, Valentine planned to send for Rosie and their two barely teenage sons, John and George. Valentine put the house in his wife's name so she could easily sell it when the time came for her to join him. But Rosie did not follow her husband, so Valentine came back to Regina to get his family. Rosie had no interest in a new start in a new country with Valentine.

Like the iron he forged, her husband was a hard man whose temper burned hot, especially when fuelled by drink. During one rage, he had set fire to most of Rosie's clothes. He became obsessed with the notion she was having affairs. Valentine often scrutinized his wife's underwear for proof of her infidelity.

But his wife proved more unyielding than the steel he hit and bent.

Mustering her courage, the battered wife turned to police in April 1926 and had her husband charged with assault. Her resolve weakened three days later. Rosie withdrew the charge the day before Valentine was due to appear in court. She even paid the $4.25 administrative cost.

Valentine's jealousy consumed him. In his twisted mind, the blacksmith began to believe Rosie was not only cheating on him but wanted him dead out of revenge for his efforts to stop her. Twice in May he sought out a doctor. Rather than blame his stomach pains and vomiting on the beer he'd been drinking, Valentine was convinced that Rosie had poisoned his morning porridge. Dr. Laurent Roy drove Valentine to the hospital, pumped his stomach and ordered that the contents be analyzed. But the sample was accidentally thrown out before it could be examined. Valentine called the doctor again two days later. The patient remained under observation in hospital for a week. But the doctor did not find any signs of poison.

Later, other doctors would wonder if Valentine's delusions stemmed from an injury suffered decades earlier on a Russian battlefield. While gathering hay in a meadow for the army's horses, Valentine had been hit by shrapnel in the forehead when the enemy opened fire.

Despite his claims that he was being poisoned, it was Valentine, not Rosie, whom the courts deemed a threat. The blacksmith hammered his wife with a washboard when she refused to give him title to the house, even though she had paid for nearly a third of it with her earnings. Two weeks later, he threatened to shoot her with a revolver—if he had the money to buy one. On June 1, Valentine was placed on a peace bond for threatening Rosie's life. Unable to find two people who would each post a $100 bond on his behalf, Valentine spent three months in jail.

His wife took the opportunity to move out.

Rosie had her new start. And it certainly didn't include Valentine. The 42-year-old woman took a suite in a rooming house. Not surprisingly, Rosie kept it spotlessly clean.

Valentine remained determined to reconcile with Rosie. Once freed from jail, he begged friends to coax his wife to return to him. He offered his wife's co-worker $25 to persuade Rosie to take her husband back. He even went to the home of a stranger, hearing that she could reunite couples. She told him to have faith in God.

Ten days before Christmas, Valentine opened an envelope containing a writ. Rosie wanted a separation and financial support. Convinced she was leaving him for another man, he began to stalk her.

Screams on Christmas night took Rosie's landlord Wallace Morrison to the second floor where his tenant lived. It was ten o'clock, and Rosie had just returned from work. Morrison found the woman shaking with fear—and Valentine scrambling to crawl out from under Rosie's double bed. Valentine, the lover, had removed his suitcoat, vest and tie, and pulled down his suspenders in anticipation of his Rosie's return.

"I'm seeing my wife," Valentine said when Morrison ordered the 48-year-old intruder to stay away. "Rosie wasn't playing straight with me," he grumbled as he was shown the door. In his rush to leave, Valentine, who had liquor on his breath, left his bottle under the bed.

Morrison saw him lurking outside the rooming house again the next night. But Valentine found the door locked this time.

The former soldier changed tactics.

He walked into a downtown second-hand shop on December 27, 1926. Telling the store owner he was having trouble with coyotes, Valentine gave a fake name to match his false story—$8 bought him a double-barrelled shotgun and shells.

From his vantage point the next day, Valentine could see the Legislative Building where Rosie worked. And his piercing blue eyes took in the sidewalk she would take to the west entrance.

Rosie and her co-workers stepped off the streetcar at Albert Street around five in the afternoon, and headed to work.

Valentine easily fit together the shotgun's barrel and stock. He loaded a single shell. But he was careful to keep the weapon hidden beneath his coat as he waited behind the parked car. When the trio turned to take the sidewalk up to the Legislative Building, Valentine emerged from his hiding place. Calmly, he walked towards the women.

"Rosie do you want to go back with me—or will I settle up with you?" he said. Seeing the gun, the women turned to flee. Rosie was still fifty metres from the doorway.

"Rosie, I shoot you," the blacksmith bellowed in German. The metal hit Rosie's lower left back, crushing vertebrae, lacerating a kidney and sending pellets through her bowel and intestine. It was the first slaying in the city of 35,000 in fourteen years. Before running off across the frozen Wascana Lake, Valentine looked back to see his wife crumpled on the ground.

Cleanliness had meant so much to Rosie. And now her blood was spilled on the pure white snow outside the Saskatchewan Legislative Building.

A rope with a noose and slip knot was found in Valentine's possession when he was arrested shortly after the shooting. Some believed he had intended to hang himself. The state would oblige him on August 26, 1927, after rejecting a psychiatric report raising questions about his sanity.

The Hold-Up

A T FIRST IT ALL SEEMED LIKE A BIG JOKE, LIKE IT COULDN'T possibly be happening for real.

It was just so weird, so surreal, and for some reason everyone was laughing. Even the woman with the gun.

"This is a hold-up," she said for a second time.

Rosaire Roy and Linda Arthur just stared at her.

They'd been having coffee at Rosaire's Prince Albert repair business, A&R Electronics Service, early one October evening when the woman came in. She was wearing a red and black devil's mask, the kind you would wear on Halloween, with her long, blonde hair hanging out the back. She was tall, and even through her sweatshirt she looked thin. Boney, even.

The woman stared at them over the counter and Linda stared back, trying to see the woman's eyes. She wanted to figure out which of their moron friends was behind the joke.

"Take all your fucking clothes off," the woman ordered.

Linda was starting to get scared. "Why?" she asked.

"Because I'm the one with the fucking gun," the woman answered. "So take your clothes off."

Linda did as she was told, slowly taking off her top, pulling down her pants. When she stopped, the woman ordered her to keep going.

"Why all of it?" Linda asked.

"No one will get hurt," the woman said. "Just do as I say."

Obediently Linda dropped her bra and underwear onto the floor amidst the piles of cash registers, faxes and answering machines in the store for repair. Rosaire was already naked, so Linda lay down on the floor with him as the woman instructed. The woman tied Linda and Rosaire together head-to-ankle with red twine. Linda's knees were on either side of Rosaire's shoulders, her legs tied loosely around his head.

As they lay there bound together, the woman rifled through Rosaire's pants and took some money from the till. Then she left, warning them not to move for twenty minutes, or someone would come back and kill them. Linda waited five. Then she reached for a pair of scissors in her briefcase, cut herself free and called 9-1-1.

TRACY BANNAB THOUGHT ROSAIRE ROY was nice. He had always been nice to her. Nice for a trick, anyway. She met him when she was working outside the Minto Apartments one day in September 2001. She was so scrawny the middle-aged business owner thought she was a boy at first, but he picked her up anyway and they fooled around. After that he became a regular, picking her up frequently, always paying for the same thing.

A month later, Roy asked Bannab if she wanted to work at his business for a bit. He said he would pay her $60 a day to make coffee, answer phones and help run the office. Bannab was thrilled. Men had paid her to do a lot of things, but never anything like that. She thought it was a really nice thing for Roy to do because she didn't like working the streets and, at 29, she'd never had a job before.

Unfortunately, it wasn't the secretarial job she had imagined.

Before long Roy told her about a fantasy he shared with a female friend, telling Bannab he wanted to be robbed and his friend, a 37-year-old woman, wanted to be raped.

He offered Bannab money to make that fantasy come true and, after some convincing, she agreed to do it. She had done that kind of role-playing before, and though her family warned against it and her boyfriend thought it was funny, she decided to take the job anyway.

Roy gave Bannab a BB gun, instructed her to get a mask and gloves, and showed her what to do once she was in the store.

Everything was planned, but when Bannab actually burst in wearing the mask, and shouting "Boogety-boogety boo" she felt ridiculous and silly. She laughed nervously, and forgot to do some of the things Roy had told her to do. He'd also told her to kick and slap and punch him, but she couldn't bring herself to do it.

And in the midst of what was supposed to be a fantasy, Bannab noticed the woman looked scared. Really scared.

It gave her a funny feeling, and as Bannab tied the naked woman up, she started to feel bad. She felt even worse two days later, when the police came to talk to her about the scheme.

The woman knew nothing about it, they said, and Roy was being charged with sexual assault. Tracy Bannab was shocked, but the discovery was most shocking to Linda Arthur, who had known Rosaire Roy since she was a teenager and counted him and his wife as friends.

Finding out that the perverse robbery had been perpetrated by someone she trusted left her reeling.

"I felt even more violated than before," she said after learning the truth.

Roy, described by one counsellor as having "a tragic mindset toward women," was given a year in jail after pleading guilty to sexual assault and falsely reporting a crime for the ill-conceived caper.

"I wish I could turn back the clock," he said, choking back tears at his sentencing.

Bannab wasn't charged because she did not know the woman hadn't agreed to the bizarre fantasy.

"And now that I think about it," Bannab said later, "it's really a rather sick thing to think about."

Linda Arthur is a pseudonym. A court order prohibits publication of any information which would identify the victim.

Brown Fall

THE PRE-SCHOOLER SNACKING ON FRESH GREEN PEAS IN THE backyard of her home had no idea her death was imminent. The bullet entered from behind, just above her left ear. Death was instantaneous. The peas she had been eating moments earlier as she played with her sister on a hot August afternoon were still in her mouth. The child didn't have a chance to even swallow.

Her death notice appeared in newspapers two days later: "Charlene Rae Friebus, 3-year-old daughter of Randy and Kim Friebus of Mortlach, died accidentally Monday evening, Aug. 20, 1990, as the result of being hit by a stray bullet."

As Rosemary Kim Friebus planned her daughter's funeral—picking a little hardwood casket, commenting how Charlene's red and white outfit would go best with it, and providing the words for the death notice—the funeral director was struck by how calm and collected this grieving mother seemed.

He wasn't alone in those thoughts. A friend noticed Kim, as most called her, two-stepping across a room just hours after Charlene's death. Another recalled her light-hearted mood the next day as she made a list, arranging the funeral as if planning a party.

Kim's demeanour seemed so at odds with what had just unfolded. But everyone handles tragedy differently. And she was no stranger to death. Charlene was her third child to die in less than six years.

KIM HAD PUT 8-MONTH-OLD Kayla to bed with a bottle. The next morning, on Halloween day 1984, the infant was blue, having inhaled fluids into her lungs. She and her sister Jamie had been back home for only three months. Kim had voluntarily placed her girls in the care of Social Services because the young mother feared she might harm them.

Randall, born a year later, failed to thrive with Kim, but flourished in foster care. The child had possible milk allergies and required special formula. In May 1986, while back in his mother's care, the 7-month-old returned to hospital—dead on arrival. An autopsy found milk fluid in his lungs. One witness told police she had seen a baby bottle taped to Randall's mouth on occasion, and blamed that for his suffocation and drowning. But police found no evidence of foul play.

Less than two months after her son's funeral, Kim married Randy Friebus. Charlene was born the following year on May 12, 1987, and apprehended within days by Social Services. She would remain in foster care for a year. With the birth of another daughter, Sabrina, sixteen months after Charlene, Social Services obtained a court order assigning a parent-aide to the family. The order expired four months before Charlene was shot.

Kim's neighbours noticed how she favoured Sabrina. Kim would welcome her youngest into her lap, but push Charlene away. Kim once slapped Charlene across the face, sending her falling into a cabinet because she started whining when Kim refused to get her a drink of water. Kim had been in one of her down moods.

With Randy working as a farmhand, and Kim, a former waitress, selling Avon cosmetic products, money was tight. By the summer of 1990, the family was seeking a referral to a food bank and buying on credit. Kim and Randy were thinking of separating. In Randy's mind, it would be temporary—so Kim and the girls could qualify for welfare.

Hoping to make a bit of extra money and study at home, Kim had begun taking a firearms repair course by correspondence. She hadn't completed it, but she had become adept at handling guns.

They also pawned Randy's .22-calibre Savage pump-action rifle several times for extra money. It was a family heirloom from his father. Three days before Charlene's death, Kim paid $185 to retrieve the gun from a pawn shop, in the hope they might find a buyer. Randy shot gophers with it the next day before tucking the rifle beneath their bed.

KIM'S NEIGHBOURS MET ALMOST daily to "coffee together" while their children played. Kim spoke that August morning of her financial troubles, and her struggle to cope. She mused about giving the children to Social Services. She used her friend's phone to inquire about welfare, saying she planned to leave her husband. The worker couldn't see Kim that day, but the desperate woman persisted and made an appointment for two days later. She also called around about selling the rifle. There were no takers.

Back at home in the afternoon, Sabrina and Charlene played outside while 8-year-old Jamie visited a friend.

It was close to suppertime when Kim, carrying her wallet, cigarettes and Sabrina, returned to the neighbour's house. She said Charlene had fallen. The girl and four pea pods lay near a bush. The neighbours thought Charlene had choked—until they noticed the pool of blood around her head. Putting her down on the kitchen table, they attempted to resuscitate her, but it was useless.

"My baby, my baby, my baby," Kim cried. Raising her blood-stained hands, she kept saying, "I've got to get this off my hands."

That night, Kim telephoned her sister and told her how Sabrina had come into the house and said, "Mommy, Brown fall." The 23-month-old was unable to say all of her sister's nickname, Charlie Brown. Kim sent her back outside because she couldn't hear Charlene crying. She watched a television show and smoked a cigarette. Sabrina returned, repeating "Brown fall." Kim looked out, saw Charlene's feet, and assumed she was playing hide-and-seek. After getting supper started, Kim found her daughter.

On the witness stand, Kim's sister would later recall how the grieving mother seemed to be in a party mood after the funeral.

"Kim is a great actress with her emotions," the sister testified. "If she thinks somebody is a very gullible person, she will put on the 'poor me' act and manipulate that person to get what she wants. Or if it's a party atmosphere, it doesn't matter what happened in that day, she's in a party mood. She switches her emotions on and off."

ALMOST IMMEDIATELY, KIM BLAMED a stranger—the shot a stray, a freak accident, her child in the wrong place at the wrong time. Within days, she blamed Sabrina, telling relatives that the toddler, who had suffered a bout of pneumonia a month earlier and was considered delayed physically and verbally, must have found the loaded gun under the bed, dragged it across her parents' bedroom and out the patio doors, shot her sister and put the gun back under the bed where police discovered it. Years later, she blamed a man, supposedly obsessed with her.

The person Kim did not blame was herself. After a jury found her guilty of second-degree murder in June 1991, she sobbed to the judge, "I didn't do it." Kim maintained her claim of innocence in a telephone interview from prison with a Moose Jaw reporter two years later. "You couldn't help but love her," Kim said in describing Charlene. "When God placed her in my lap, I knew the mould was broken."

The jury wanted Kim's parole eligibility set at less than the minimum. The judge couldn't oblige, and Kim was sentenced to life, with a chance to seek parole after ten years.

What the jury never heard was a confession, ruled inadmissible, Kim had made to the RCMP following her arrest. The 29-year-old mother of three deceased children initially said she had dropped the gun, and it went off. Then she said she was shooting at a rabbit and missed.

But it was her last, cold account—when Kim said she "just lost it"—that investigators believed was likely closest to the truth: Sabrina had begun crying because Charlene took her peas away from her, Kim said. Angry at Charlene and wanting to stop Sabrina's piercing cry, Kim took a single bullet from off her dresser. She pulled her husband's hunting rifle out from under their bed and loaded it. She opened the patio doors, stepped onto the deck and took aim, intending to frighten her child. Kim called out Charlene's name. In response to her mother's voice, Charlene started to turn, but she was stopped by the bullet.

An Area of Insanity

G OD, SHE WAS BEAUTIFUL.

She had been a tomboy when she was younger, a nice girl from a mining town with short-cropped hair and a boyish quality, but she'd grown up recently. She'd softened, matured, developed a sort of sensuality she didn't have before.

Innocent still, but with an undercurrent of something more. She had changed, and people were noticing.

One young boy from the United States had even been sending her letters—letters that started out talking about God and ended up talking about filth—but Robert didn't mind. He knew she was his. They would marry, start a life together, spend their lives as one.

She wrote him beautiful songs that promised him so.

"I needed you and you were there," she'd sing to him, repeating the songs over and over again so he knew she meant it. "And I'll never leave. Why should I leave? I'd be a fool, 'cause I've finally found someone who really cares."

He did care, and when she talked like that, he knew she did too. He knew they would be together forever.

The world didn't believe him, of course. Not the lawyers, the judges, the psychiatrists, the media—no one understood how much she loved him. Not even, it would seem, Anne Murray herself.

At first Robert Kieling wasn't sure if anything would happen between them. She was, after all, Canada's sweetheart, a pop princess and international music star, and he was just a farmer from Blumenhof, a working man with a 320-hectare wheat field a couple hours west of Regina. It would be understandable if she didn't feel the same way he did.

So he sent her a letter. Just to see. He even included a handful of wheat seeds from his farm as a simple gift.

She wrote back to him.

From there, Anne became the primary focus of his life. "A textbook case of erotic paranoia" one psychiatrist called it, the unshakable belief that a famous person is in love with you.

And believe it he did.

Kieling created a hallway shrine to his love, complete with a silver-framed publicity photo, flowers and candles. During a concert in 1977, he jumped up on stage and grabbed her, embracing his Anne desperately until security dragged him away.

Three years later, he faced his first criminal charge for intimidation, and received a stern warning to have no further contact with Anne. He wouldn't—or couldn't—comply.

After that came a series of court battles that would span the decades, as Kieling continually broke court conditions not to contact the singer, and regularly wound up in jail because of it. He didn't care.

He called Anne collect from the Regina Correctional Centre while he was awaiting trial, appeared on her doorstep within a week of getting out of jail for harassing her. There were periods when he phoned her office several times a day and hundreds of times a month. He repeatedly showed up at her home in Toronto and at her mother's house in Nova Scotia, and was once sentenced to two months in jail for attending one of her concerts in Regina. He went to her high school reunion, her father's funeral, and sent her presents that included a $500 diamond ring.

"Your situation is becoming pathetic," a judge told him frankly in April 1985.

But Kieling wasn't prepared to take all the blame. They had a hot and cold relationship, he said, and Anne liked to make trouble for him. Something to do with her childhood fantasy of being an actress.

"She's sort of a bizarre person, that's why my behaviour is bizarre," he said. "She's a mischievous person who likes to play games."

She would send him secret messages hidden in her songs and album covers, he said, and once dispatched the Snowbirds aerial flying team over his house as a secret message to him. He suggested he may even be a dupe in a ploy to boost Anne's ratings.

"When people think I'm insane they probably have a legitimate reason to believe that, based on the basis of the information they have," he admitted. "But it's absolutely incorrect."

In December 1987, Kieling invited Anne to take the train to Swift Current and spend Christmas with him, advising her to bring along the Bible and *Fall of the Titans*, the 1954 novel by Soviet defector Igor Gonzenko. She didn't come, but Kieling never gave up.

His obsession led to more than five years in jail, several stints in psychiatric hospitals and countless hours defending himself before the courts, experiences he described as "almost Kafkaesque."

And while the doctors may have words for it, for those who knew Robert Kieling, it was much harder to understand. He was an educated man who gave generously to charity, loved hockey and classical music, and spoke French and German. Even police who arrested Kieling described him as a quiet man who never resisted their authority. He represented himself in court with determination and aplomb, and won occasional battles on points of law. As one psychiatrist said: "If one removes this disorder, Mr. Kieling appears to be a very normal person."

But then there's Anne. There's always Anne.

"He thinks I should be able to understand," said Kieling's elderly mother. "I said to him, 'This is what I understand, this is what's real: She has charged you, sent police after you and she isn't lifting a finger to get you out of trouble. And that tells me she doesn't care.' This thing is destroying my son. It isn't normal that he doesn't stop, we have to agree to that. But it's not a question now of whether he's right or wrong, it's a question of helping him."

But Kieling never wanted help.

"How many people's private lives would seem bizarre if they were absolutely exposed?" he said. "Every person has an area of insanity in their lives."

Loyalty, Trust and Truthfulness

THE GUY IS CALLED Q-TIP, AND THEY FINALLY FIND HIS CAR parked outside a strip club in Vancouver. Paul and Dave sit in Dave's truck, watching as Q-Tip buys a case of beer and gets into his Trans-Am. Then they tail him to a hotel in Burnaby, hanging back a bit so he doesn't see them.

"This guy must be stupid," Paul says.

There's no other word for someone who owes the Mafia twenty-five grand.

"I love doing this shit," Paul laughs, rubbing his hands together in anticipation.

At the hotel, Paul knocks on Q-Tip's door and asks for Sarah. Then he goes back to the parking lot to tell Dave that Q-Tip's alone.

Dave grabs the wooden fish bat he bought earlier that day, and they go back to the room. While Paul stands watch outside the door, Dave pushes his way into the hotel room to deal with Q-Tip. The moment the door clicks shut things go crazy; Paul hears yelling and banging, a chair being knocked over, something hitting the wall.

When Dave finally calls Paul into the room there's blood everywhere and Q-Tip is down on all fours looking bad. Dave kicks Q-Tip in the stomach, pours a beer on Q-Tip's head, empties his wallet.

You have one day to get the money together, Dave warns. Or you're fucking dead. He tosses the bat at Q-Tip as he and Paul walk out of the room.

Paul laughs as they drive away from the hotel. "He knew," Paul chuckles. "When he seen you he was scared."

Dave is excited by the beating he gave Q-Tip. It's a rush to do that, and he tells Paul it kind of turns him on. Paul likes it too.

"We are a lot the same," Paul says.

The two men met in January 2001 at a Grizzlies game in Vancouver, after winning free tickets to the NBA game in a beer promotion. As part of the prize they and the other winners were picked up in a limo and got to eat and drink for free while watching the Grizzlies play the Miami Heat. It was a great night, and Paul and Dave hit it off right away. It seemed they had a lot in common. They exchanged phone numbers and Paul started doing some work for Dave a short time later.

THE FIRST JOB IS SIMPLE, just a matter of driving a van full of American booze to a pub in Whistler, but Paul does well. He did some driving for the bikers a few years back, and he doesn't mind if a job isn't legal. In fact, he prefers it.

When Paul finds out Dave is hooked in with a big organization from down east, he wants in.

With Dave vouching for him, Paul is quickly trusted with bigger jobs, like moving a truckload of handguns packed in cubes of pink insulation to a prospective buyer.

As they pull away from Q-Tip's hotel that night, Paul says he can do even more for Dave's organization in the future.

"After we get the money we should fucking whack the guy," he says. "I can do more than knock on a door."

Paul and Dave are cruising through Abbotsford in Dave's hot new Camaro one afternoon in April when Dave gets a call from the boss. He wants to meet Paul. It's an important meeting. There's a big deal coming up, and Paul could make $25,000 if the boss likes him enough to let him do the driving.

As they head for the meeting, Dave gives Paul advice. Be truthful. The boss hates lies, so don't try to bullshit him. Don't try to impress him by saying you did something you didn't do.

The boss especially wants to know about a teenager who disappeared ten years earlier. Paul was arrested for it once, and even though he was never charged, his name is still on an RCMP file about the case. The boss is worried this is a loose end that will score too much heat, but if he can get the details—and he likes Paul enough—the boss will make sure that stuff goes away for good.

When they walk into the condo, the boss is sitting on the couch sipping a glass of red wine. He's wearing a suit and tie, looking relaxed on the plush red couch. He's not menacing, but he's not someone you'd want to be messing with, either. He tells Paul to relax.

"You work for us, we'll protect you, " he tells Paul, his voice rough with hints of an Italian accent. "You will not go to jail."

So Paul tells him the story.

He says this 19-year-old kid, Gordon Spears, came to stay with him and his wife in Edmonton a long time back. The kid was in big trouble. He'd seen a member of the Asian gang Lotus shoot a guy in the head over a coke deal in Vancouver, and he was the key witness in the case against the shooter. The gang members didn't want him to testify so they sent him to Paul's place.

The kid's father reported him missing in October 1992, three days before the trial was supposed to begin.

The kid was supposed to live at Paul's for only three months, but he stayed there for more than a year, spending his days sleeping on the couch, drinking beer, smoking joints and playing with Paul's young son.

When the Asians got sick of paying for the kid, they gave Paul a handgun—and an order.

Paul told the kid he was being moved to a new hideout in Saskatchewan, and they drove out of Edmonton on a cold December day with the kid hiding under a blanket in the back seat. Paul stopped near Pierceland and the kid got out of the car.

"I put a bullet right in his fucking heart," Paul tells the boss.

"You shot him in the heart," the boss repeats.

"Fuckin' right," Paul says.

But Paul's story doesn't jive with information the boss got from one of his RCMP sources. When Paul and Dave leave the meeting and get back in the car, Dave knows Paul has lied to the boss. He pounds the steering wheel and swears. He vouched for Paul, so Paul's lies look bad for him.

Paul asks to go see the boss again.

Back in the condo, Paul apologizes.

"My fear is from the Chinaman to my children because they don't care about killing kids," he says.

"Don't worry about the Chinaman," the boss says, "Don't fucking worry. As I trust you, you trust me. Nobody, nobody is going to bother you. Ever again. You come with us, we fix you up."

So Paul tells his story again. Most of it is the same, until the part where he pulls out the gun. This time he says the kid dropped to his knees on the ground begging for his life.

"Whack, I shoot the guy," Paul says. "I hit him in the head."

Not in the heart like he said before, in the head. Straight through the star on the front of the kid's baseball cap.

The boss forgives Paul's lie this time, but warns it can't happen again.

"When you belong to us, you belong to us 24/7," he says. "I come before your wife, your kids, your fuckin' dog or even your cat. I call for you to come help, you come."

"Absolutely," Paul says.

"With that loyalty, that trust and that truthfulness you will not have no problems," the boss promises.

PAUL IS ON HIS WAY to meet Dave on the afternoon of April 20, 2001, when he is arrested in the alley behind his Maple Ridge apartment and charged with the murder of Gordon Spears.

Only then did Jean Paul Joseph Aubee know he had been the target of an RCMP sting operation, carefully planned and orchestrated to illicit a confession in the decade-old murder of the British Columbia teenager.

The operation began four months earlier, when two representatives of a beer company knocked on his door and told him about a beer contest. The beer company reps were police officers, the contest was a setup. All of the other winners—even the limo driver—were cops playing a part in Project Expire.

Paul's friend Dave was not a friend at all. He was an undercover police officer who kept extensive notes on all their conversations and reported back to the RCMP immediately after every meeting. The jobs Paul and Dave did together were phony, even Q-Tip and his beating were part of the act. The "boss" was an experienced RCMP officer, the condo an elaborate stage set concealing a video camera and microphones.

It was all fake, Paul would come to realize.

The only things that were real were his videotaped murder confession and the sun-bleached skull of the man he killed—found in the brush near Pierceland, a single bullet hole right through the forehead.

The Boy Who Wanted To Fly

SOMETIMES, WHEN SANDY WAS SCARED AT NIGHT, HE imagined the sound his wings would make, the feeling of rising up above his town and looking down on all the people there.

A sickly child pestered by ear infections and pneumonia, Sandy Charles approached his 14th birthday as a lanky, pale-faced boy with scraggly long hair and droopy eyes. He didn't have a lot of friends at school, and instead preferred to spend time with his best friend Mark, an 8-year-old kid who lived nearby.

Though Mark was much smaller and younger than Sandy, some people in town thought the two boys looked alike, with long wavy hair and similar faces, but in personality they couldn't have been more different. Sandy was quiet and shy, Mark was brash and bold—stealing, swearing, berating a neighbour who sometimes took pity on him and gave him lunch when his family wasn't around.

AT FIRST, NO ONE EVEN KNEW Johnathon Thimpsen was missing.

His grandmother wasn't surprised when the 7-year-old didn't come home that Saturday evening, and figured he was probably staying somewhere else for the night.

She called the RCMP the next evening.

For two days, residents of the small, northern community of La Ronge scoured the area, looking for any sign of the young boy. On Tuesday, July 11, 1995, shortly before 7:00 p.m., five volunteer searchers made the gruesome discovery in a small grove of bush and trees.

It was a sight that would disturb even the most hardened investigators. That small body. Unrecognizable.

It wasn't hard to catch Johnathon's killers, of course. They were just children. Police arrested Sandy two days later and charged him with first-degree murder. Mark was too young to be charged.

THE IDEA CAME FROM A 1980s horror movie called *Warlock* which was popular with kids in La Ronge around that time.

Sandy had watched the movie a lot, and especially liked the parts about witchcraft. He figured what the movie showed was probably true, but said he double-checked it later in an encyclopedia while working on a report about suckerfish.

"It said nail and fat and all that gives you powers and things," he told police.

He had been thinking about it for a long time, watching the movie over and over, but he told Mark about it for the first time on a warm summer day in 1995, as the two stood in their La Ronge schoolyard.

Mark wasn't sure at first, but Sandy was adamant.

If you drank the fat of an unbaptized virgin you could fly, he promised, the movie said so. And there were other secrets, too. Powers you could get, Sandy said, like if you ate a human heart, and someone came towards you with a knife and you said stop, they'd stop because you'd be so powerful.

That's what Sandy told his best friend in the schoolyard.

And that's when the two boys started picking a victim. There were plenty to choose from. Most of the kids they knew were unbaptized, probably all of them were virgins. Mark and Sandy tossed around some names, kids at school that might be good. They almost decided on one boy from Mark's class, but they couldn't be sure.

On July 7, 1995, the day after Sandy's 14th birthday, the two were hanging out at Sandy's house when they chose Mark's cousin instead.

The next morning, Saturday, Sandy got everything ready. He took one of his mother's paring knives, and pulled the label off an empty soup can. He hid both of the items in a bush behind his house, then he and Mark invited Johnathon Thimpsen to play baseball.

IT WASN'T LIKE THE movie at all.

In real life it was a lot harder to kill Johnathon than Sandy thought it would be.

After luring Johnathon into the woods, Sandy had tried to break his neck, but couldn't. He stabbed the boy in the head a few times and hit him with a beer bottle, but even that didn't work. Finally Mark passed Sandy a big, heavy rock, and Sandy hit Johnathon with that. Then he covered Johnathon's nose and mouth with his hands until the boy quit breathing.

"It was gross," Sandy said, recalling the murder. "I didn't know blood would come out."

But there was blood, and lots of it—so much blood that Sandy almost couldn't go through with it.

"I wanted to stop after I had him down," he said. "But Mark was saying, 'You deserve it Johnathon.' And Mark was happy, I know because of the look on his face. He wanted that stuff. I wasn't happy. I was kind of scared."

When it was all over Sandy told Mark to go get a towel, which Sandy used to wipe the blood off his face and hands. Then the boys snuck back into Sandy's house, and Sandy washed his clothes and the towel while Mark left to return a movie to the video store for Sandy's mom.

After about an hour, Sandy took a second knife and a

pair of kitchen tongs and went back to the body to get some fat.

"Sandy cutted off around ten pieces," Mark told police.

Sandy melted the fat down in a soup can on the stove at his mother's house. He was going to do it over a fire outside, but had heard that too many fires were destroying the ozone layer.

Then Sandy had a shower. Cried. Hid the can in the basement.

"I didn't want to drink that stuff," he said. "I just wanted to stay the way I am."

But who was he? Sandy had been confused about that for a long time.

To others in town he was a quiet boy, somewhat unremarkable. He delivered newspapers, babysat his younger brother, and got average grades. There were some signs of concern, of course; his friends were always much younger than himself, and he'd been withdrawing lately, becoming quiet and strange. At school he wrote bizarre and violent stories, and he was becoming increasingly obsessed with germs and needed to use different forks for different food.

Sandy had heard a long time ago that he was haunted by the evil spirit of a relative—his great-great-grandpa, or maybe a great-great-great uncle. Sandy thought the man used to kill babies or something, but he always forgot the story. All he could remember was that it was an evil person who did some evil, evil things.

"If you're the devil's son you're supposed to help him," he said. "That's what I thought before I was going to drink that. That it was almost the year 2000, and that would have been real bad 'cause I would have had to help him or something."

Then there were the threes. Threes everywhere. He was 3 the first time he saw the devil, and his family used to live in a haunted apartment that was #303. His house was haunted by three spirits. He dreamed about three trees that could take you someplace else.

It was a feeling that had been building through the years, he said, something cold that sucked him backward into darkness.

And the devil. Standing in the bathroom when Sandy was a boy, smiling at him. A black thing in the corner of his eye, a male voice waking him up in the middle of the night asking, "Are you listening, Sandy?"

Sandy was.

But standing in that clearing with Johnathon's blood on him was different. And when it was all over, Sandy knew—though he would later forget—that he had done something terribly wrong.

"It was evil," he said. "I knew it was bad after that. Something was encouraging me before I did that, and after that everything went away."

For a while, anyway.

But while in prison—where he was being tested to see if he would be held criminally responsible for the murder of Johnathon Thimpsen—some of the old feelings came back.

Sandy began getting angry. He didn't like being there. The lights were burning him, and he had to shower eight or ten times a day to cool off. He made himself bleed then drank his own blood. He thought he might be growing vampire's teeth.

When he dreamed about killing people, he would wake up laughing. Always laughing.

"Sandy never cries for anyone," his mother said.

Sandy wanted to leave. And there were ways to do that, Sandy knew.

Things he could do to fly far away.

Sandy Charles was found not criminally responsible for the murder of Johnathon Thimpsen and was committed to a psychiatric hospital. Mark is a pseudonym. Because of his age at the time of the murder, he was identified only as "M." After the killing, he was sent to a foster home.

Blood Relatives

QUIETLY EYEING HIS PREY, ALLAN TOCHER STOOD AT THE doorway. Perhaps it was just a chance meeting, but Tocher's next move was very deliberate. He strode back out to his girlfriend's pick-up truck, pulled his hunting rifle from the cab, and went inside the farmhouse. Pumping the lever on his Winchester, Tocher ejected four bullets onto the linoleum kitchen floor.

"There are still five more," he said, making sure his audience knew the gun was loaded and ready. They were just as sure no one crossed Allan Tocher.

Roy Wiggins, an oil rig worker, had come to the farm north of Manor on June 29, 1994, to visit friends. He counted Tocher among them. Until tonight, Wiggins didn't even know he had become Tocher's enemy. Travelling with his girlfriend, Helena Twigge, and his 18-year-old son David, the gun-toting Tocher was not on a social call.

"We were on the way to town to cut your mother's throat and shoot you," he told Wiggins. Then the 46-year-old bully topped the brutal threat. He said he would first castrate him, "one nut at a time."

The source of Tocher's anger became clear moments later.

"You got a half-hour left to live, to think about what

you've said," he menaced. "The police were at my place, and told me that you ratted me out." It's uncertain if Tocher was telling the truth or simply trying to confirm his suspicions.

MONTHS EARLIER WHEN THE two men were doing time in jail, Wiggins had told his cell-mate that he wanted to get rid of his wife. He asked for Tocher's advice, believing his friend had some experience in this area.

RCMP weren't even aware Tocher's wife Lavina had vanished until December 1991, when they received an anonymous call. By then, the 35-year-old troubled wife and mother had been gone three months. Hers was a marriage plagued by alcohol and drugs. Daughters Penny and Sherry accepted their father's story that Lavina had simply opted to leave. Then a police raid on the Tochers' Parkman-area farm in August 1992 turned up $200,000 worth of marijuana plants, as well as Lavina's purse and identification. It did not look as though she had just packed her bags and walked away.

In June 1994, Wiggins brought a hitman with him to Tocher's farm to pick up a few more tips on wife-killing. Two days after the trio's last meeting, Tocher was done giving advice. Now he was planning a murder—not the slaying of Wiggins' wife, but of Wiggins himself.

The hitman Wiggins had brought to Tocher's farm was an undercover officer. RCMP wanted information about Lavina's disappearance, and Wiggins had agreed to help.

RCMP would later swear in court that no Mountie had tipped Tocher off about their informant. But Tocher certainly believed his former friend had committed the unforgivable. He had ratted him out to police.

TOCHER, HIS SON, AND TWIGGE took turns taunting Wiggins as he sat at the kitchen table inside the home of Twigge's younger brother. Tocher offered Wiggins his gun, Twigge a butcher knife—making him think he had a chance. But Wiggins knew how the game was played. Tocher told him to go ahead and shoot. "I'll still come over there and pull your windpipe out," he said.

A drunken and distraught Twigge levelled her own accusations. "You raped me," she charged, claiming 45-year-old Wiggins had sexually assaulted her twenty-five years earlier when she was a teenager.

Twigge called Wiggins a coward because he wouldn't take the gun offered by her boyfriend. Grabbing a bottle of whiskey by its neck, she threatened to hit Wiggins over the head. But even if Tocher didn't think much of the man sitting before him, he valued a good bottle of rye.

"Don't waste it, it's Wiser's," he told Twigge.

For nearly two hours, Wiggins endured, hoping for an escape. When the friend who had brought him to the house rose to leave, Wiggins tried to join him. But the hunted man barely made it past the table. Tocher stopped him with a punch to the face. The friend heard Wiggins' head smack the floor. Then he left—alone. Twigge warned him not to say anything.

He drove away and did as he was told.

Tocher's rat remained trapped. Wiggins was driven to the home of Tocher's brother-in-law, who found the bullet-riddled body later that night blocking the porch door. The smell of gunpowder still hung on the air. Wiggins had been shot in the head, neck and abdomen—seven bullets from two different rifles.

Rushed on adrenaline, the father and son bragged to 15-year-old Sherry and 14-year-old Penny about having just killed a man. Flesh from Wiggins was still on their running shoes.

At Penny's home, a subdued and withdrawn Twigge paged through photos of her eldest son. Seven months earlier inside the Tocher farmhouse, the 16-year-old had lifted a rifle to his mouth. He was playing and assured Twigge it wasn't loaded. He pulled the trigger. She watched her son die.

Both Penny and Sherry could see the fate of their brother and father. The men had come to say goodbye. Tocher had spent too much time behind bars and was not about to do anymore.

ON CANADA DAY, MOUNTIES hiding in the poplars had their guns trained on Tocher's weather-beaten farmhouse. They knew the father and son were alone inside. Twigge had already been arrested at her home. At first, the Tochers had responded to the RCMP's calls. But then there was dead silence.

The next day at four in the morning, RCMP brought the thirty-three-hour siege to an end. Tear gas filled the home. Police went in prepared for a gun battle that did not happen.

Officers pushed back a two-by-four barricade on the upstairs bedroom where Sherry and Penny used to sleep. The father and son lay dead. Each man had put his rifle between his legs and fired under his chin, into his own head.

The Mounties wondered about other lives that could have been lost. The Tochers had eight firearms and a large cache of ammunition.

Twigge was the only one alive to be put on trial. She was initially convicted of first-degree murder for aiding and abetting the killers. After an appeal, a second jury found her not guilty. Unlike the first trial, Twigge had taken the stand and said she was in her truck, sleeping off the effects of booze and marijuana when the Tochers let loose their revenge on Wiggins.

Twigge's acquittal came a week before the fifth anniversary of Lavina Tocher's disappearance. RCMP still consider her a missing person. But some people believe they already know what became of the woman who once so loved Allan Tocher, she defied her parents to marry the man nine years her senior when she was just 15 years old.

As the Tochers threatened Wiggins, David let slip the fate of his mother. He said she had been put through a wood shredder and fed to the pigs.

A Snake Around His Heart

THE PLATFORM AT THE ROSTHERN TRAIN STATION WAS crowded that morning with relatives, neighbours, and friends. Excitement and curiosity mingled with grief as they waited in the cool autumn air. At last, the train from Prince Albert pulled into the station, and the crowd caught sight of the woman in the dark muskrat fur coat. Her black, silk headshawl made it difficult to see her attractive face or the expression she wore. But the child recognized her immediately. The little girl broke free from the crowd and ran towards her mother. The youngster, about 5 years old, was one parent shy of being an orphan. The next few hours would help determine if the remaining half would also disappear from her life.

KATERYNA WAWRYK WAS REALLY just a child herself when she became Kateryna Tracz at the age of 14. Her husband Jakim was considered a good catch, at least Kateryna's parents had thought so. Nearly eleven years older than his betrothed, Jakim was an established farmer in the Fish Creek district when the couple wed at the turn of the century. During twenty-three years of marriage, the child bride grew up alongside her eight children, who taught their illiterate mother to read and write when she was well into her 30s. Kateryna loved her children.

She felt something else for her husband.

Jakim had left his son to work the fields the morning of October 9, 1923, while he went to town to pay some bills. He covered the thirty miles to Rosthern and back with his team of horses hitched to a democrat wagon. It was close to sunset when Jakim got home. Kateryna had supper waiting.

The family sat down to meat rolls, sour cream, tea and cookies. Kateryna slipped away from the table and returned with the brown bottle of home brew. The family owned only one glass, and she filled it from the brown bottle and set it on the table in front of her husband. Jakim ate his meat rolls and sipped his whiskey.

Almost immediately, Jakim felt as if a snake had wrapped itself around his heart. His children watched their father tremble and fall face forward onto the kitchen floor. He was in agony.

"Wife, what have you given me?" Jakim demanded.

"I have given you the same as the rest," Kateryna replied innocently.

As the searing pain overtook his body, Jakim knew she was not being honest. A school board trustee, he sent his 16-year-old son William to ask the teacher, who lived nearby, for help.

William Hooper arrived to find Jakim convulsing on the floor, and helped him onto the sofa. He left his wife Lena at Jakim's side when he drove off in his automobile to get the doctor.

Lena Hooper made a mixture of mustard and ginger, which she poured down Jakim's throat. He did throw up. But not enough. "I'm burning up inside," he moaned.

Their neighbour Sophie Kalynka also came to help. But Jakim knew he was well beyond it. "Wife, wife, why did you not give me water? Why did you give me poison?" Klynka heard him say.

The realization that his wife had betrayed him most certainly hurt, but, at that moment, it paled compared to the excruciating pain tearing through every muscle of his body. "Why did you not give me a bullet?" he called out.

Two hours had passed since Jakim had sat down to supper with his family. The convulsions were worsening, and Jakim's limbs were rigid. Mary, the only one of his children Jakim would see wed and start her own family, arrived in time to watch her father take his last breath.

The bell atop the Greek Orthodox Church rang out to let people know about Jakim's death. The 48-year-old father and grandfather was buried on the Thursday.

Kateryna had been arrested one day earlier. It was not unexpected—but the arrest of Theodore Oleskiw was.

THEODORE AND HIS WIFE ALEXANDRA and their infant son Joseph—the first of eight children—had, like Jakim, immigrated to Canada from Eastern Galicia. Theodore's success and reputation grew over the two decades since his arrival in Fish Creek. At the time of his arrest, the carpenter and farmer who spoke several languages and could read and write English was considered a community leader: a councillor for the rural municipality, a former reeve, and chairman of the school board. He had buried his wife, who succumbed to pneumonia and blood poisoning, that February and seen his eldest married in the spring. His son Mike was also thinking of marriage that October. He was seeing Tekla Tracz—Jakim and Kateryna's daughter.

While the lives of the two families became intertwined that fall, it was not through marriage.

Kateryna had been at the Oleskiws in October to help with the cooking during threshing. Later, some of Kateryna's children would remember Oleskiw dropping her off at home three days before Jakim's death. Tekla, also called Tillie, was certain she saw her future father-in-law give her mother a little white package.

"I poisoned him," Kateryna confessed to her family as her husband's body was laid out beneath a sheet in the sitting room. But she didn't stop there. Kateryna said she had not acted alone. "I did it for the love of Oleskiw," she told her family, and later the constable who came to investigate.

Kateryna told a courtroom that Oleskiw, still handsome and well-built at 48, had promised to marry her when her husband was gone. "I wanted to kill my husband because Oleskiw was kissing me and telling me we were going to live together," she said. "But I did not want to poison my husband. I was ready to go with Oleskiw and leave my husband and children."

Oleskiw was, in fact, engaged to another woman, a wealthy widow from Cudworth. They were to marry once threshing was complete.

Kateryna swore Oleskiw had given her a bottle of strychnine and told her how to put it in her husband's home brew. She sweetened the poison with a bit of sugar, masking its bitterness.

Each year, the rural municipality provided its counsellors with strychnine to put on wild land and school yards to take care of the gophers. Oleskiw had received ten bottles. At his trial, Oleskiw did admit giving Kateryna strychnine—but at her request, not his. It was for killing gophers, not her husband, he said, insisting she was crazy and he knew nothing of her homicidal plans.

KATERYNA'S YOUNG DAUGHTER followed her into the town hall that morning. She hadn't seen her mother for a week since her arrest and stayed at her side until the proceedings got underway. The hearing would decide if there was enough evidence to try Kateryna for murdering her husband. There was. And much of it came from the mouths of Kateryna's own children, who recounted their father's dying words and repeated their mother's confession. In February 1924, Kateryna Tracz was convicted of murder and sentenced to hang. The same children who had condemned her helped spare her from the hangman's noose by petitioning the government. Her sentence was commuted to life, and she was released from prison in June 1938.

As Kateryna's trial concluded, Oleskiw's opened. She took the witness stand against the man she believed would marry her with Jakim gone. Her words carried no weight with the jury.

"Thank you, my lord. Thank you, gentlemen of the jury," Oleskiw said upon hearing the not guilty verdict.

Two months later, Oleskiw's son Mike married Kateryna's daughter Tekla. However, Oleskiw's plan to marry the widow from Cudworth was not to be. She broke off the engagement.

Maybe the jury did not believe Oleskiw had helped poison Kateryna's husband, but she certainly poisoned her co-accused's reputation. And it was equally bitter. The gossip and innuendo were insidious, like a snake closing in on its prey. The venomous court of public opinion proved too much for Oleskiw. Four years after his acquittal, he put his land up for sale and left the area.

Whiter Than Mine

THE TWO MEN MET ON A BEAUTIFUL JUNE DAY IN THE SUMMER of 1982, completely by chance. If the car hadn't broken down, they would simply have passed each other somewhere on the road near Kenaston, each man speeding to his destination without any consequence at all.

But the car did break down. And because it did, Joseph Duffy and Robert Ironchild met on the side of a long Saskatchewan highway, under that vast and clear summer sky.

Duffy, a respected professor at the University of Regina, was pursuing a doctorate in education at the University of Alberta at the time, and had been commuting regularly between his temporary residence in Edmonton and his home in Regina.

He was on his way to Regina that day, and, after a brief visit with an old friend in Saskatoon, the 51-year-old drove south out of the city on Highway 11 in his yellow Pontiac Lemans, excited to get home to his wife.

As it happened, Ironchild was also in good spirits that day. He had a bit of money, and was looking forward to his 27th birthday the next day. It was the first time in several years he'd been out of jail for his birthday, and he was hoping for a good party.

Ironchild left Regina that morning with his friend Brian Obey, Brian's girl, Simone Dubois, and Brian's cousin, Germaine Obey. The group packed Ironchild's car with plenty of beer, whiskey, marijuana and a cat. On the way out of town they stopped at a gas station to buy junk food and batteries for a portable tape player. They also bought a knife.

The first part of the trip was great, with everyone laughing and talking as Ironchild sped down the highway, but somewhere between Regina and Saskatoon the car stalled, and Ironchild pulled over to the side of the road. Everyone in the car was laughing, but Ironchild didn't find it funny at all. It looked like the engine was blown.

"Go get your sexy legs out there and catch us a ride back to Regina," he told Dubois.

She tried, but no one wanted to pick up four people. After a few cars passed without stopping, Ironchild was getting annoyed. He hid in the ditch, promising Dubois he would shank the next honky that came along.

When Joseph Duffy saw the woman alone on the roadside and stopped to help, Ironchild sprang from the ditch and jumped into the car with the knife drawn. Pushing his way into the driver's seat, Ironchild turned Duffy's car around on the highway and pulled up to his own broken-down vehicle.

While his friends moved items between the two cars, Ironchild demanded Duffy's wallet, then grabbed Duffy's eyeglasses and threw them out the window.

"You won't be needing these in the future," he said.

As the group drove down the highway, Ironchild threatened Duffy, berating him, calling him names and saying he was going to kill him. He said he hated honkies, and told Duffy all white guys think Indian girls are cheap and easy. He stabbed Duffy in the thigh, then yelled at Duffy to stop bleeding. The professor begged for his life.

"Take everything I have and leave me alone," he pleaded. "Don't kill me, please."

Ironchild wasn't listening. Instead, he pulled off the highway and onto a gravel road, then headed toward a cluster of empty farm buildings in the middle of an open field. Pulling into a shed, Ironchild told Duffy to get out of the car. Duffy was trembling, shaking his head.

"No, please, just leave me alone," he said. "Promise me you're not going to do anything to me."

Ironchild screamed at him to run.

Duffy did.

He ran straight into the field then turned into the granary, with Brian Obey chasing him on foot and Ironchild trying to hit him with the car. Ironchild nearly hit Duffy once, but missed, which enraged Ironchild even further. He chased Duffy around the shed again and again with the car, missing him by inches each time before finally running over him in the field.

After Brian got back in the car Ironchild hit the gas, heading back to the highway in a cloud of dust. The girls tossed Duffy's identification out the window.

A few minutes later Ironchild stopped for a young man hitchhiking along the road. A university student working a summer job in Weyburn, Terry Gibson was hitching to Saskatoon to see his mom and brother, and was thankful to see the car pull over to pick him up. He climbed into the back seat with the women.

Things were pleasant for a few miles, everyone in the car chatting casually, until Ironchild and Obey pulled out knives and demanded Gibson's money. Ironchild's knife was covered in blood, and he told Dubois to lick it off. She did, at first with her tongue, then dragging her finger along the blade. She looked at Gibson as she put her finger in her mouth.

"I love the taste of blood," she said.

Ironchild started looking for a place to pull off the highway. They told Gibson they were going to take him onto a grid road, slice off parts of his body and kill him.

Gibson told Ironchild he was scared.

"You're not nearly as scared as you're going to be," Ironchild promised.

When the car slowed down to turn, Gibson jumped out of the moving vehicle and rolled into the ditch. Then he ran across the road and threw himself on the hood of a passing vehicle to get the driver to stop.

While Gibson went to call the police, Ironchild continued on to Saskatoon, where the group had lunch and coffee with Ironchild's mother. Dubois and Brian Obey hitchhiked back to Regina that night. Ironchild drove back to Regina with Germaine Obey the next day, dropping off the car with Ironchild's half-brother, who crumpled it with a bulldozer then set it on fire.

Duffy's mangled body was discovered two days later by a farmer and his children. The professor died face-up in a field of tall weeds, a bloody handkerchief clutched in one hand.

Police arrested Ironchild a week later, finding him in the living room of an east Regina house with two superficial, self-inflicted wounds on his neck. He was mumbling about a car accident he had been in two years earlier, and about the loss of two of his children.

While he was recovering in hospital, Ironchild told RCMP Sargeant Ronald Squire he remembered very little about the man he met on the road that day.

"Do you remember what colour his skin was?" the officer asked.

"Whiter than mine," Ironchild replied.

When asked why he had run over Duffy, Ironchild said it was to get his car.

"You already had his car," the officer pointed out.

"I know," Ironchild said.

Then Ironchild got tired of answering questions.

"I'd like to take a piss," he told the police officer. "If you got some more questions hurry up, I'd like to sleep. I'm guilty. I'm being straightforward. When a guy flips he flips."

*Ironchild, who later changed his name to Rob Wapuchakoos, was convicted of first-degree murder, and sentenced to life in prison without any chance of parole for twenty-five years.

Top Dog

GARY GILLINGWATER WAS OFTEN SEEN PEDDLING HIS BICYCLE around town. With his knapsack in tow, the bespectacled man with the rust-coloured comb-over didn't cut much of a swath. And that was okay by Gary. He liked his privacy.

No one in Fort Qu'Appelle knew he was the Top Dog. At least, not until the gossip spread, travelling faster than the river that winds through the scenic valley.

Had he confined his travels to these quiet streets, Gary would have continued to live in relative obscurity—at least outside the small town where he already stood out. But Gary found cruising on his computer even more enjoyable, maybe obsessively so. With the Internet, he explored far beyond the modest bungalow he shared with his longtime male lover on the outskirts of this conservative community of two thousand. His cruising took him to the The Eunuch Archive, a Web site based in Florida.

That's where Gary, the chain-smoking, 57-year-old former chef, became Top Dog—although admittedly he was really more of a cat lover. Sometimes, he preferred the handle Cutter Canada. On the Web site dedicated to the human equivalent of turning bulls to steers, Top Dog had the gonads to get the job done. He had been doing human castrations for twenty-five years, he boasted. The Web site brought Gary and Terry together.

Terry wanted to be neutered, and Top Dog wanted to help.

But while Gary bragged about his expertise, in reality he truly was not on the cutting edge of the procedure. His experience was limited to watching his brothers castrate farm animals in his youth. But Top Dog was, well, dogged in his determination. He knew you could learn almost anything from the Web. The old Dog tried to learn a new trick.

TERRY AND HIS MOTHER CHECKED into the hotel on the edge of Fort Qu'Appelle around suppertime on May 11, 2001. When Gary knocked on the door of Room 102, he brought his package. Inside a flowered-patterned tissue box, Top Dog carried what he guessed he would need: scalpel, scissors, gauze, and tape. The only thing missing was anaesthetic.

Eager to put an end to the hormonal poison that flowed into his body from his testicles, Terry lay back on the bed as Gary took stock. Taking the scalpel in hand, Gary sliced through Terry's scrotum, removed the testicles, cleaned the wound, and stitched it up. Two hours after he had arrived, Gary left with his tissue box, a fistful of $20 bills, and Terry's testicles.

"Oh God," Terry's mother heard her son say an hour later. And he wasn't praying. There was blood running down Terry's leg and pooling on the floor. The 28-year-old Calgary-area man was hemorrhaging. He was rushed by ambulance seventy kilometres away to a Regina hospital. An actual doctor successfully finished the job begun by the man who would earn a new name the next day on the town's coffee row—Dr. Gary.

QUIET, SOFT-SPOKEN, UNASSUMING Gary received e-mails from people across North America and Europe. There were others like Terry wanting to take advantage of Top

Dog's services. Like Terry, some had grown frustrated with the long process required to undergo a conventional sex change. Gary e-mailed back to say he was out of business.

Seasoned Judge Kenn Bellerose had presided over everything from murders to shoplifting. This was definitely a first. "It's not every day someone loses their privates," he said.

Gary pleaded guilty to unlawfully causing bodily harm, but he swore he meant well. The ugly scars on Terry's genitals were proof of previous crude attempts to affect the change he so desperately desired. "I just wanted to help," Gary told the judge. That's why he charged only $100. Bellerose put the first-time offender on probation for eighteen months with strict instructions to stay off the Internet.

Almost two months before Terry met Gary in Room 102, a curious posting appeared on the Web site that had brought them together. "Have two nice balls to be removed soon," it read under the general castration discussion forum. "Yours for a minimum of $300. Shipped to you in preservative or frozen. No bull, no pun."

Terry's testicles were never recovered. But the Top Dog in the town that owes its start to a trading post denied having peddled them.

Terry is a pseudonym. A court order prohibits publication of any information which would identify him.

The Hunter and the Hunted

THEY NEGOTIATED A DEAL FOR $20 EACH. BONNIE CLIMBED into the back seat of the grey Mercury Cougar, and went off with the two strangers to a motel.

Leaving Bonnie and his friend in the room, Bill took a walk. He returned when John was finished with the woman.

"Go ahead," said John, as though he were inviting someone to take a turn in a board game or have an extra piece of cake.

Alone in Room 165 with Bonnie, Bill assured the woman he would pay her—but he would not touch her. "As far as he's concerned," Bill said of his friend, "we did it."

"Keep your mouth shut," he added.

Bonnie, shivering in the cold motel room, pulled her clothes back on. The two bided their time.

"Can I give you some advice?" Bill asked Bonnie as they prepared to leave. "Don't go with him alone if he tries to pick you up again by himself. 'Kay? That's between you an' me."

John was a little surprised when his buddy exited the room so quickly, but Bill assured him he'd had his money's worth. After dropping Bonnie off at Lucky Buck Bingo, the two longtime friends returned to the motel and settled in to watch television.

But Bill clearly had something on his mind.

"Why the fuck did ya take 'em to the same place for … jeepers." He paused, then continued, "I thought you'd take 'em somewhere else."

"They made me mad," said the sullen, tight-lipped John.

"What?" asked Bill.

"They made me mad. I killed 'em first," John said.

"Then you drove 'em out there?" Bill asked.

"Yeah. Then I dragged their bodies into the bush," added John.

Bill, not one to let the conversation lull, chuckled, "I thought after that first one you wouldn't fuckin' go near that goddamn place at all."

"That was the safest place to put 'em," John said.

Moments later, John asked his friend, "You know that cement place?"

"Killed 'em there," John added. "That's where it happened. One yelled—one was gonna yell rape. An' I said, 'You ain't raped. I pay you good.' She said, 'No you did-n't. You didn't pay me enough.' I says, 'Oh yeah.' An' I choked her."

"Which one was that?" asked Bill, eagerly digging for more details. "With the bra strap? Or the other one? … With the glasses? Eva?"

"Yeah," was John's only reply, but he offered more later.

"This one here," he said, pointing at a picture in the newspaper. "I did it there at the bushes there. I jus'—I took her into the bushes. We were sniffing, and I hit her over the head with a …" John's voice trailed off.

Bill tried to pick up the story. "Yeah, that's the one with me an' you."

John corrected his friend. "No. That's another one."

Later, Bill tried to get it all straight. "Okay, so the one

with the glasses an' long hair. You did over, down over here. An' the one that's in the paper, you did out in the field."

"Yeah," said John.

"Okay. Whew. Like I said, you got more balls than a brass monkey. Fuck. I'm tellin' ya' man. I wouldn't a had the fuckin' balls doin' her over there." The two buddies shared a laugh.

Before leaving to make his curfew, John and his friend made plans for the next night. Bill would call John's house, but wouldn't leave his own name so as not to tip off John's mother. She had never liked Bill. Always protective of her son, Victoria Crawford believed Bill was constantly getting him into trouble.

She was half right.

Her son certainly was in trouble.

Bill's help had guaranteed it.

As on the two nights before, the conversation between John Martin Crawford and Bill Corrigan on January 14, 1995, was caught on tape—by the body pack Corrigan wore, the listening device in the car Crawford borrowed from his mother, and the bug planted in the couch at the motel room paid for by the RCMP.

Corrigan, the 43-year-old chatty criminal-turned-informant, would collect $15,000 for his efforts. He and Crawford had first met in prison about seven years earlier. Crawford had been serving time for manslaughter. Renewing their acquaintance outside prison walls, they often went out together to drink and pick up women in Saskatoon.

The unsavoury ex-con became the best hope of ensuring that Crawford would never again be free to kill. Without the tapes and Corrigan's eyewitness account of one woman's death, there was little to link Crawford to the murders of three women.

Their families never saw them alive after the fall of 1992. For two agonizing years, they were left to wonder.

CALINDA JEAN WATERHEN WAS A slender 22-year-old who never got to see her baby girl grow up. A hunter was scouting for deer when he stumbled upon Calinda's sun-bleached skull on October 1, 1994. Her bones were scattered in heavy bush southwest of Saskatoon near Moon Lake.

Known locally as Bare Ass Beach, it was the ideal summer spot to drop your clothes, if you were so inclined, and enjoy the sun. Crawford made it his dumping grounds.

A rebellious 16-year-old, Shelley Gayle Napope had vowed in letters home that she was going to straighten out her life about a year before she disappeared. Her large, dark eyes were her most striking feature, but it was her prominent overbite that allowed an anthropologist to put a name to her corpse. Shelley's skeletal remains were found three weeks after Calinda's and about thirty metres away.

A Mountie combing the underbrush found Eva Taysup's shallow grave the very next day. She had been rolled in two blankets, secured with an orange electrical cord. Just a few years earlier, the 28-year-old woman would have tenderly wrapped her own four young children in their blankets. Unlike the other two bodies left exposed above ground, Eva's remains largely escaped the ravages of carnivorous animals roaming the area.

None of the disadvantaged First Nations women were originally from Saskatoon. But alcohol, family circumstances, and misery had drawn them to its downtown bar and street scene. They became easy prey for Crawford.

What remained of the women told nothing of how their lives had ended. But Eva had suffered a fractured jaw and broken rib around the time of her death. And her left forearm had been sawed off before she was buried.

Corrigan first told RCMP in October 1993 about a woman named "Angie" who was killed at Bare Ass Beach. Back then, the Mounties were paying Corrigan to gather information on illegal cigarette sales. Police doubted the validity of his tale when they failed to find a body.

But the Mounties were eager to speak to him a year later.

Until Shelley was identified, Corrigan had always thought the young woman he and Crawford had picked up in 1992 was "Angie." The trio drove to Moon Lake in a beat-up Chevy Nova Crawford often borrowed from his mother when he went hunting for women. Crawford ordered his friend out so he could have some privacy. Hearing a scream, Corrigan looked back to see Crawford hitting and choking Shelley. They were having sex when he looked again.

Corrigan lit up a cigarette and turned away.

Shelley was crying and had a split lip when Corrigan returned to the car. The frightened teen wanted to go home and promised not to press charges. But Crawford insisted they were going to have sex again. Then he would take her home. Shelley's dark eyes pleaded with Corrigan.

"Don't look at Bill. He's not going to get involved," Crawford told her.

With Crawford pulling on Shelley's arm, the naked young woman got out of the car and walked towards the bushes. Corrigan saw her doubled over, as though his friend had punched her in the stomach. Crawford dragged her further into the bush. A scream brought Corrigan closer. He saw Crawford with a knife in his hand, and Shelley dead on the ground.

"I killed her," said John, who enlisted Corrigan in covering Shelley with branches and leaves.

Corrigan was unloading groceries from Victoria's car sometime later when he spotted women's clothing stuffed into the trunk. Crawford said he planned to get rid of them. "What's one more?" he reportedly told Corrigan.

That was not the only evidence Crawford destroyed. The buck knife used to kill Shelley had belonged to Corrigan. During the taped meetings at the motel room, the informant repeatedly asked about the fate of his knife. Crawford assured him he had dropped it into the Saskatchewan River.

CRAWFORD'S MOTHER COULD NEVER understand why her gentle son had said the things she heard on the tapes. He was still her "good boy" even when the 32-year-old convicted killer was charged with slaying three more women. As a child, Victoria's eldest had been a slow learner who was self-conscious about the scars on his chest and neck—a lasting reminder of playing with a cigarette lighter at age 4 while in the care of a babysitter. He also claimed he'd been molested as a child by a female sitter. This may have explained his difficulty relating to women with the exception of his mother. He lived in her home until his arrest five days after his last damning conversation in Room 165. Victoria visited him in jail no fewer than twenty-six times in the months before he was sent to a federal prison in May 1996 for the first-degree murder of Shelley and second-degree murders of Eva and Calinda.

Crawford had never testified at his trial. He was afraid the prosecutor would "tear me to shreds." But for his appeal—which ultimately failed in 1999—the killer had plenty to say in a self-serving affidavit. As much as he tried to diminish his guilt, Crawford's sworn statement betrayed his ruthlessness.

Eva was the first to die, he said. They met in September 1992 at a bar and headed to the "cement pond"—an industrial cement factory—to have sex and drink beer. They dined on pizza pops and chocolate milk at a convenience store before returning to the factory a second time. The sun was beginning to rise when Eva asked for a ride back into town. According to Crawford, she wanted $150 for three sex acts. He thought $50 was enough because he had supplied the booze. When she threatened to "yell rape," Crawford grabbed her by the throat.

"I remember thinking, 'she's only worth $50. I'm not going to jail. She has no right to live.'" Even when she went limp, he kept his hands on her throat to make sure she was dead.

"I remember thinking, 'Oh shit—nailed for another murder.'"

Crawford put Eva's body in the trunk of his mother's car and drove to Moon Lake. He had originally planned to cut up all of her body, but decided after sawing off her lower left arm that it would take too long.

Crawford thought he had killed Calinda the very next day. Almost seven years later, he couldn't be sure. The two picked up dinner at the KFC before driving to the cement factory to eat and drink booze. Calinda wanted to sing along to the radio while they had sex in the backseat of his mother's car, Crawford recalled. As with Eva, he insisted Calinda wanted more than the $45 he offered. She threatened to go to the police—perhaps because it really was rape and not the pleasant, consensual deal Crawford claimed. He choked Calinda to keep her from talking.

"Fuck, there goes another one," he thought. She too went limp beneath his grip. Once again, he returned to Moon Lake to abandon a naked body beneath leaves and branches.

He and Corrigan picked up Shelley about a week later. Crawford said he had sex with the teen first by Moon Lake, then left Corrigan and Shelley alone in the car while he went off in the bushes to get high sniffing lacquer.

Crawford thought at first it might be nice to have a girl to sniff solvents with and get high together, but decided it was a bad idea. "I tend to get into fights with people when I sniff," he recalled. Contrary to what his ex-buddy had to say, Crawford claimed Corrigan killed Shelley in the bushes because she wanted $200. In Crawford's version, Shelley already had a gash across her throat when he stabbed her eighteen more times—to see if she was dead.

"I wondered if she was just playing dead."

THE JURORS HAD NONE OF THAT information. Nor did they hear from two other Aboriginal women who said they were attacked by Crawford in 1992. One was choked unconscious and raped near a cement factory. A hitchhiker said Crawford had agreed to drive her home—then took her out of town, raped and choked her. A third woman, shaken and with her pants undone, emerged from Crawford's car in October 1994 while RCMP had him under surveillance.

The jury also did not know Crawford was an experienced killer, having served half of a ten-year manslaughter sentence in prison. He was 19 years old when Mary Jane Serloin met him in a Lethbridge, Alberta bar two days before Christmas in 1981. Her nude body was found nearby in a back alley. Crawford claimed the 35-year-old Aboriginal woman had begun choking while they were having sex, and was bruised when he tried to revive her. But he had left his bite marks on Mary Jane's cheek, neck and breasts. She had also suffered severe internal injuries. While she lay dead or dying, Crawford returned to the pub for beer and pizza.

Crawford's idea that women were easily used, easily disposable began at an early age. He had his first sexual encounter when he was 13. He and two other boys paid an 11-year-old girl five bucks for sex. It was a one-time thing, Crawford told a psychologist years later.

Perhaps, that's also what he told himself after slaying his first victim.

Justice David Wright sentenced Crawford to life in prison—and he meant it. He said the serial killer should never be freed. By law, parole ineligibility had to be set at twenty-five years, regardless of the number of stolen lives. "I would make it longer if I could," the judge said of the most disturbing case he had presided over in his sixteen years on the bench. Wright was struck by the contempt and brutality with which Crawford had treated Shelley, Eva, Calinda, and Mary Jane. "He seemed determined to destroy every vestige of their humanity. He left three of them naked, and lying on the ground.

"There is a kind of ferocity in these actions that reminds me of a wild animal, a predator."

A predator whose crimes might have gone undetected, if not for a hunter.

In his book Just Another Indian, *author Warran Goulding suggests Crawford is a prime suspect in the unsolved murder of another woman, whom he was charged with sexually assaulting in 1992, and in the disappearance of two others.*

Friendly Fire

Dennis O'Connor arrived at his best friend's house late one November evening in 1986 and got some very bad news. Brian Schultenkamper was dead. He'd been shot — killed by a sniper with a single bullet. The assassin had shot Brian through the window of his cell at the Regina Correctional Centre, hitting him in the abdomen and severing a major artery. The 21-year-old bled to death.

Hearing the news, Dennis sat down on the couch and wept.

Brian's mother Violet could not comprehend why anyone would have targeted her son.

"I don't know why and I don't know how, but he was shot," she sobbed. "That doesn't make any sense, does it?"

Of course, Brian Schultenkamper did have his problems. Most seriously, there was Russell McMurty Emmerson. The elderly war veteran had asked Brian back to his place for a drink a few months earlier, and was found dead in the apartment later, the knife still sticking out of his back. Brian had been charged with murder.

In jail before his trial, Brian was depressed and anxious. He told friends he was being set up for the murder, and a nurse at the jail suggested he see a psychiatrist.

And while Brian's death may have been a surprise to

his mother, it wasn't the first time someone had tried to take his life. He'd narrowly escaped being killed while serving time on an earlier jail sentence, when he was stabbed during a fight with another inmate.

Still, Dennis, who was living with the Schultenkampers at the time of Brian's death, didn't know why anyone would possibly want to kill his best friend. Or at least that's what he said.

He was arrested and charged with murder later that day.

DENNIS KNEW IT WAS A bad idea from the beginning. It seemed incredible that the plan would work. How could you shoot someone in the stomach and not kill them?

But Brian was insistent.

Dennis had to shoot him and it had to be serious. Brian had to be injured badly enough to be taken out of the jail for medical treatment. He had to get to a hospital and once he was there, they'd plan his escape. It was dangerous, Brian admitted, but more than likely he'd survive the shooting and it would be easy to break out of the hospital.

They'd tried unsuccessfully to break him out of jail in the past, so Brian believed this was the only way. Eventually, Dennis came around. He told his neighbour about the plan over a drink one night.

"Wouldn't that kill a person?" Ed Yanoshewski asked, as they sat in Ed's living room.

"No," Dennis said. "Not if you shoot him in the stomach."

During one of Violet's weekly visits with Brian, he gave her a note to pass along to Dennis. It was folded and Violet didn't look at it before delivering it to her son's best friend. She should have.

"The time has come my friend," Brian had written to Dennis. "Too much time has been wasted already. Please for both of us, don't fail me... It might be dark in here and hard to see, but one must do what one cannot do."

So Dennis did what he could not.

On the evening of November 6, he armed himself with a powerful .303 Lee Enfield rifle he'd stolen from the father of one of his friends, and loaded it with aggressive soft-tipped bullets. He had planned to use steel-tipped bullets, which cause less damage, but he couldn't find any. The plan had already been delayed when a jailbreak put the facility into lockdown, and with Brian set to stand trial in four days, it could not be delayed again.

Dennis went to the jail outside Regina. He knew the place well; he'd been serving time there for armed robbery when he met Brian.

Crouching low to avoid being seen, Dennis cut a small hole in the chain-link fence around the jail grounds and crawled through on his stomach. Creeping up to the building in the dark, he found the window Brian had described in his note—Cell 11 in the West G wing.

With his heart pounding, Dennis smashed a window near the basement-level cell and poked the barrel of the gun through the bars. Brian jumped off the bunk.

"He's here and he has the gun," Brian excitedly told his roommate, Donald Favel.

The news sent Favel scrambling under his bunk, and he hid there scared and praying.

The bullet burst into the room with a deafening crack, a flash of light and shattering glass. Brian fell to the ground moaning.

Favel knew that he was hit, and was afraid to see how bad.

Dennis saw. He watched as his friend gasped and fell backwards under the force of the bullet, and the blood began to flow. Then Dennis ran away, leaving the gun behind him.

The jail came immediately to life. Prisoners screamed and shouted, chanting "flush the bullet." Heeding the cell block's instructions, Favel scrambled to find the bullet fragment and put the evidence down the toilet while guards rushed into the cell.

Brian was on the floor, blood gushing from his stomach. He was dead by the time he got to the hospital. Doctors tried to revive him for twenty-five minutes anyway.

Just less than a year later, Dennis went on trial for murdering his best friend.

Despite the efforts of defence lawyer Gerry Allbright—who argued Dennis should only be convicted of manslaughter because he didn't know the shot would be fatal—Dennis O'Connor was convicted of second-degree murder and sentenced to life in prison.

"Brian was going to do fifteen to twenty years and now I'm going to have to do his time," he told a police officer after his arrest. "I only did what he told me. He said if I didn't do it he would slash himself up and come back and haunt me."

Football, Fowl Suppers, and Funerals

THE AFTERNOON WAS SPENT SHOOTING AT CARDBOARD targets in a gravel pit. Afterwards, David Hares and Robert Gulash settled in with friends to watch the football game on television. The Saskatchewan Roughriders were playing the Winnipeg Blue Bombers in their push to eventually gain a spot in the Grey Cup.

At his home less than an hour's drive away, Joseph Helfrick was also cheering on the Riders. But Porky—as he was known to his friends—had to tear himself away early. The local elevator agent put on one of the two suits he owned.

For years, the Catholic Women's League had hosted a fowl supper in the basement of Our Lady of Grace Roman Catholic Church at Sedley. The feast typically drew just over 400 people—about a hundred more than lived in the town. Porky had volunteered to handle the ticket sales in the church vestibule. As her father got into his car to head to the fowl supper on October 17, 1976, Bonita Helfrick ran to tell him Winnipeg had just scored a touchdown.

In Regina, Gulash lost interest in the action on the television screen. He pulled out his handgun and showed it off to his friends. He even let one of them touch it. Gulash liked his .22-calibre, snub-nosed revolver. Bought a little over a week earlier in a downtown bar, the gun's serial number had met with a hacksaw blade.

No one could remember exactly how the conversation turned from football and guns to fowl suppers. But as the talk went on about the annual fall feasts, hunger grew. Hares, Gulash and Janet Vance, Gulash's girlfriend of a couple months, had little but booze in their stomachs. A phone call confirmed there were three suppers in the area. Sedley was closest.

At the Lajord road sign, Hares pulled his car over so he could relieve himself. Gulash used the pit stop to fire four shots into the sign.

It was around 5:30 p.m. and already more than 300 tickets had been sold for the supper when Hares, Gulash and Vance walked through the church doors. Hares bought the $3 tickets from Porky and Eddy Leier. Joining his friends in the second pew, Hares gave Gulash his change before stretching out and throwing his feet over top the front seat. The brazen show of disrespect from the 22-year-old stranger drew a few stares in the largely Catholic community.

Fifteen minutes later, the hungry friends watched eagerly as a man stepped up to the microphone to announce the football score and inform ticket holders up to the mid-hundreds that they could head down to the supper. Realizing they would have to wait for some time, with ticket numbers near four hundred, the trio decided to head back to Regina. Eddy refunded Hares his $9.

As Gulash steered his friend's Monte Carlo out of town, Hares, in the backseat, mentioned the cash box. He figured there was about $1,000. "Nice chunk of money," Gulash agreed. The church could be an easy target, because there weren't any RCMP in town, he added. It was the voice of experience.

The 34-year-old electrician had gone to prison seven years earlier for robbery and abduction. His girlfriend's pleas to halt their scheme went ignored. Gulash's eyes hardened.

No more was said, but the two men looked at each other in the rearview mirror. They nodded in agreement, and Gulash turned the car around.

Pulling into an alley by the church, Gulash took his gun from the glove box and loaded five rounds into the six-shooter.

In the church vestibule, the gunman pulled the revolver from his pocket, and pointed it at Porky. At first, the ticket sellers thought it was a toy, someone's silly prank. But when the thief scooped up the little green cash box and tucked it under his free arm, they knew the gun was real.

"You'll never get away with it," warned Porky.

Later, townsfolk easily recalled the red hooded jacket worn by the bearded robber. Many believed the gunman was Hares, who had been wearing the jacket when supper goers spotted him sprawled out near the front of the church. Some even noticed the nasty cut over his eye, suffered in a hockey game two days earlier.

Gulash, a seasoned criminal, and Hares, a hardware store clerk whose only trouble with the law was for driving drunk, were an unlikely match. But with their long dark hair, full beards and moustaches, the two looked remarkably alike. Although Gulash was slightly taller, they were about the same weight and build, so occasionally swapped clothes.

Before re-entering the church, Gulash had borrowed his friend's red jacket in hopes the hood might cover his face.

"Get the hell out of here," Gulash shouted as he climbed into the passenger seat.

Porky and Eddy jumped into their cars to pursue the robbers. With speeds reaching 130 kilometres an hour, three other vehicles driven by fowl supper diners joined the chase. Hares, who was driving, spotted the cars in his rearview mirror and told Gulash. The gunman looked back. The vehicles were gaining on them.

Eddy's car made contact with the Monte Carlo's rear bumper. Gulash rolled down the passenger window and fired four shots. He would later insist he had only wanted to scare the other drivers. It seemed to work. Eddy backed off initially. But a kilometre up the road, he tapped the robbers' bumper again. Eddy dropped back, but began to close the distance a third time.

Gulash loaded four more bullets into his gun, and told Hares to stop the car. Thinking he could keep the robbers from going forward, Eddy pulled his car up on the driver's side of the Monte Carlo and parked at an angle. Porky stopped immediately behind his friend. Gun in hand, Gulash walked over to Porky and yelled at him to get out of his car. Porky instead pushed down the lock on his door. An enraged Gulash fired one shot through the windshield at the steering wheel. Porky slid over to the passenger side, opened the door and stepped onto the grid road near Vibank.

Elbows bent, Porky had his hands up as he walked to the side of the road. Gulash held the gun's hammer down and followed behind. A single shot entered Porky's back, fracturing a rib, collapsing a lung and slicing into his liver. The bullet cut a hole through his plaid sports coat and left gunpowder on his flesh. The revolver had been fired at close range—no further than an inch away. The 54-year-old husband and father of three grown children lay bleeding to death in the shirt his wife had washed and ironed that afternoon so he could wear it to the supper.

Witnesses swore they saw Porky and Eddy standing together, hands up, at the side of the road with a gun pointed at their backs—execution style. A 13-year-old girl out horseback riding remembered four men on the road. She was hiding behind some farm machinery when she heard the shots.

Gulash claimed Porky was already down when he turned his attention to Eddy and ordered him from his vehicle. The 50-year-old farmer's life ended with a single shot, the bullet entering near his right ear. With his head resting on his hands, Eddy lay in the dirt as he had sat minutes earlier in the church—at his friend's side. His wife, still cleaning up at the fowl supper, was unaware she had just lost the father of their three sons.

The other pursuing vehicles arrived just as the Monte Carlo fled. Real Coupal rushed to the men. Porky turned his head. "Real, I just won't make it," he said. Eddy was already dead. Porky's words proved prophetic. He died en route to hospital.

Three hours after they had first walked into the Sedley church, the trio was back at their rental house in Regina, counting money, downing drinks, and awaiting delivery of a pizza Vance had ordered.

As RCMP sketches of the two wanted men made the news the next day, Hares and Gulash tossed the gun, holster and cartridges in a slough. They stuffed a few of the stolen bills into their pockets, and gave the remaining $1,056 a shallow burial near some willows in the countryside. Their getaway continued to Saskatoon in Gulash's car. They were on their way back to Regina that same night when RCMP stopped the vehicle at a roadblock.

At their trial, Gulash blamed a hair trigger, Porky's supposed attempt to grab the gun, and a slip on the gravel road—theories rejected by the Crown, an RCMP weapons expert and more importantly twelve jurors who found both men guilty of first-degree murder. They were sentenced to life in prison, but Hares got a break on appeal. His conviction was reduced to second-degree murder with parole eligibility after ten years.

For Gulash, it truly was a life sentence. He died of cancer before becoming eligible for parole.

At the trial, Bonita Helfrick was asked if she recognized the suit coat with the gunpowder residue as the one her father had worn. She was quite sure when she pulled an invitation from the breast pocket. It was for a wedding held four months before the fowl supper, also at Our Lady of Grace Church. At the time of her father's death, Bonita was herself engaged to be married. Her father would have walked her down the aisle. Instead, she attended his funeral. More than 800 people—twice as many as went to the fowl supper five days earlier—filled the church for the funerals of Porky and Eddy.

Two days before, another grieving family gathered in a Regina church. They were there for the funeral of a 13-year-old boy who was hit and killed by an unmarked RCMP cruiser hours after the fowl supper. The vehicle had been heading to an apartment building in the hunt for the Sedley Supper killers as the boy crossed the street.

Compounding the senselessness of the night, the tip about the suspects' whereabouts was wrong.

Of Death and Survival

THE RIFLE WAS POINTED AT HER HEAD WHEN SHE CAME TO ON her kitchen floor. "You're faking it. Get up you bitch," said the man at the end of the gun.

Emma never knew from day to day what was going to happen when he came home. If she would be beaten—again. Fear was the only constant in her life. He had a way of hurting her that didn't leave a visible mark—a punch where her clothes would cover or ripping hair from her head. Emma changed her hairstyles to conceal the bald spots. Sometimes, Max didn't care who saw the blackened eyes or broken teeth. He liked to kick or throw her about the room. The only thing she fought back was her tears. If he heard her cry, he hit harder.

After the beatings, Max would expect her to make love to him. It was his way of showing that he forgave her for the bad she had done—whatever had made him hit her. Sometimes Emma thought about leaving. However, Max checked the mileage on the car before and after he went to work. If he beat her for leaving dirty dishes, what might he do if he discovered she had taken the car? No one defied Max. Certainly not Emma.

She usually tried to hide her mistakes before Max got home. But this time, the 18-year-old who once thought she was in love with this man had done the unforgivable. She had left a burnt pan on the stove to soak.

Emma blacked out when he knocked her into the cupboard. Lying dazed at his feet, she begged him to spare her life. "Don't shoot me. I'll be good. I won't leave a pan on the stove again," she said. He must have believed her. Max didn't shoot.

But there were times later in their relationship when Emma would wonder if she had done the right thing. Maybe it would have been better if he had pulled that trigger.

Like when Max watched from the shadows as she had sex with his friends. It was easier to give in to his bizarre demands than to suffer the consequences of not doing so. If Emma just lay there and closed her eyes, it would be over in minutes. A beating could go on for a week.

Max had spared her life, but she tried to take it. At first Emma thought it was just another of his sick jokes when he mentioned the dog. Years later, she could not remember how it started. But she would never forget what followed. Her head pinned between Max's knees. The dog behind her. It was like she was in one place, and her mind somewhere else, watching from a distance. Emma couldn't live with the memory. Three times, she tried to kill herself.

MEMORIES TORTURED RITA, TOO. She was only 10 years old the first time Max touched her. They were coming back from the store when he pulled his pickup truck over to the side of the road and pinned her against the seat. Max told her he was helping her mature faster with his kisses and groping. He promised it would not happen again. But it did— and it was worse. Max believed he had a duty to teach Rita, a virgin, "the ropes." If she did not bend to his will, he threatened to hurt those she loved. Maybe next time he would use his work boots a little harder, he said. Or he could bring along a mouse or a snake to scare her. Once he had put a mouse down her shirt. She was terrified. Max laughed.

For five years, he had his way, raping Rita. The more she fought, the rougher he got, biting, pinching and pulling her hair. Besides, no one would believe her even if she told, Max convinced the school girl. Rita disappeared within herself. No one could know what had happened.

EMMA AND RITA PUSHED their secrets deep inside them—as did the others. Yes, there were others as well. Six were children when Max stole their innocence. Enid was raped five times. The 13-year-old tried fighting back, but the heavy-set Max would put his hand over her mouth and take what he wanted. Still, she always blamed herself.

A master at manipulation, Max lured some of the children with the horses he treated just as harshly as he did the women in his life. He liked to pinch and tease, but the children overlooked that for the chance to ride a horse. Once Max had the girls alone, he molested them.

His step-daughter Judy used to think of Max as a father, until she was 12 and the abuse started. Then she felt like his wife—there to cook, and clean, and service him. For seven years, she endured, numbing her body to his touch while taking her mind away somewhere else. Somewhere safe.

The women believed they suffered alone. At times, doubts crept into their dark thoughts, and they shuddered to think there might be others like them. Then the guilt, the shame, the humiliation, and the fear would rise. The secrets got pushed a little deeper. The children—grown to adulthood—tried to move on. But the secrets, though buried deep, returned as nightmares and made them feel uneasy in the arms of their own husbands decades later.

Gloria was 12 years old when Max raped her after she had come to his home to babysit. It was not the only time. Max told her it was her fault, and she believed him. He was the adult, after all. Like the others, Gloria tried to forget.

After almost twenty-five years, she could no longer

hold back the memories. They pushed into her conscious-
ness and terrorized her as much as they had at the time.
But no longer was she a child cowering from a bully.
Gloria shared her secrets with police. No longer alone, the
others told, too. Once victims, they had become survivors.

"I found a lot of brave, courageous women," said
Gloria after they had taken the witness stand against Max.

BETWEEN 1964 WHEN HE STARTED with Emma and 1983 when
he finished with Judy, James Yanoshewksi—known to
most as simply Max—wreaked havoc in the lives of eight
women. He tore families apart, created mistrust, and
instilled insecurity as he victimized partners, relatives,
babysitters and family friends.

"James acted as a predator, pursuing his own sexual
gratification with those who were too young and too weak
to resist his advances. The only limit to his sexual appetite
was opportunity," Justice Ellen Gunn said before sending
him to prison. Max was convicted of two physical assault
charges and ten sex offences, including one count of forc-
ing a woman into an act of bestiality.

The women watched as Max was taken into custody
after the verdict in November 1994. "We're safe. We can go
on living from here," said Rita. She and Gloria felt as
though they had been granted their freedom, released
from a prison. It was a feeling Max himself would not
experience.

Declared a dangerous offender, Max was ordered to
remain behind bars until such time as a parole board
deemed he was no longer a risk to society. That day never
came. The man who had once wielded such power and
control was helpless against the disease that ravaged his
body. Max could not beat cancer. He died in a prison hospital in 2005 at age 61.

*Emma and Enid are pseudonyms. A court order prohibits publication of
any information which would identify them. The other named women*

requested the court not shield their identities. Some, like Gloria, felt they didn't want to hide, while others worried banning their identities might prompt the court to conceal Max's name because of their relationship to him.

Art and Avarice

WITH ITS PANORAMIC SCENE OF GONDOLAS ON A CANAL and the basilica in the background, the oil painting captured the beauty of 18th-century Venice. The Italian masterpiece, along with an equally valuable Van Gogh and a Dutch work reputed to have once hung in Budapest's Royal Palace, was among dozens of paintings donated to two Saskatchewan art galleries. Hard-pressed to find the money to buy such valuable works themselves, the curators could not believe their good fortune.

In honour of two of the donors, highly regarded physicians, the Moose Jaw Art Museum held a gala exhibition in the fall of 1974. "We have tried to collect a varied group of fine European masters and excellent Canadians to balance our collection," read a brochure for the opening. "Let us hope the future generations value these as much as we have." Members of government, the mayor of Moose Jaw, and other local celebrities attended the event.

At the centre of the philanthropic achievement was Joseph Olah Jr. The Regina art dealer had a knack for forging relationships between galleries and wealthy donors. Doctors, dentists, a pharmacist, a lawyer, entrepreneurs and business owners—the best of citizens, in the words of the lawyer's wife—became his clients. What they lacked in an art education, they made up for in taxable income.

They soon learned donations of art were eligible for a tax deduction. If the work was a gift to the Crown—and then loaned to the galleries—the write-off was 100%. The paintings would have to be appraised, of course, and that's where Olah could help.

Considered a knowledgeable art dealer, Olah was known to have evaluated paintings for insurance purposes. In his youth, he had taken a few university classes in art history, but had no degree. Most of his training came from his father, who had been an art dealer for nearly five decades since emigrating to Canada in 1957 from Hungary. Olah also had a reputation for getting his hands on fine pieces of art at fire-sale prices during buying trips to Europe.

A Regina surgeon had already bought two paintings for $14,000 when Olah suggested someone of his standing should really donate something more valuable. And that's how the Moose Jaw Art Museum ended up with the Venice canal scene bearing the signature of the Italian master Canaletto. The surgeon had paid $25,000 for the fine piece. It was, admittedly, a large sum, but he had been assured by Olah of its value. Indeed, the art dealer appraised the work at four times its price. But after reading a book about Canaletto, the surgeon began to worry he'd been cheated. Canaletto's works were selling for three or four times Olah's appraisal. The middle-aged, middle man went back to the gallery—and returned with a $250,000 receipt for the doctor.

The surgeon thought it best not to question how Olah might have obtained such a valuable painting at a cut-rate price. Another Regina physician had let it slip that Olah's father had once worked for a large museum in Budapest and brought out valuable paintings after the war.

And so everyone came out ahead—Olah got paid for the paintings; the galleries received pieces of art; and the donors got a tax break. And their generosity would not go unnoticed. Their names were engraved on plaques hanging in galleries alongside their donated artworks.

But the paintings also caught the eye of the taxman, who was losing thousands in potential revenue from the doctor and the other art buyers. A year after the Moose Jaw gala art exhibition, the federal government and RCMP were investigating.

They got a second opinion on the doctors' donated art.

The 18th-century Canaletto had not been painted by the master. It was in the style of one of his lesser students, but not even a good likeness at that. The painting, valued at $250,000 and purchased by the doctor for $25,000, had been bought by Olah for $1,339 at an art auction in Amsterdam. At best, it was worth $2,000, according to the head of the appraisal division of the esteemed Sotheby's of London and New York.

A landscape bought for $130 was appraised at $58,000 for the doctor, who donated it to Saskatoon's Mendel Art Gallery. It did, after all, have a signature that read "Vincent," in the style of Van Gogh. The only problem, according to the expert, was that the signature had been added years later. The painting was worth $300.

A lawyer had paid close to $13,000 for three paintings that also went to the Mendel. Olah appraised them at $49,500. They were actually worth $550.

The Amsterdam art broker recalled that Olah had bought about 200 fifth-rate works from him between 1969 and 1974. He usually paid a couple of hundred dollars— and appraised them for thousands

But Olah did not restrict his expertise to European art. A landscape, sold as a work by James Henderson, did indeed have a link to this Canadian artist. "Balcarres Coulee" had been painted by his housekeeper, who parted with the oil painting when Olah kept pestering her. She had refused to give him her genuine Henderson, a gift from the artist for her years of service.

Instead of being shown at other gala exhibitions, more than a hundred paintings became court exhibits. The trial judge could not help but notice that Olah often appraised the paintings for nearly exactly his client's net taxable income. The works of art were originally purchased between 1973 and 1975 for about $17,000 and sold to the donors for $117,000. While the expert placed their value at about $35,000, Olah appraised them at $941,500, to the tax advantage of his clients.

Olah, along with two doctors and a druggist who were part of the art-for-tax scheme, was sent to jail. "I am not sentencing doctors, a pharmacist and an art dealer, but criminal conspirators who were running a massive operation based on their and other people's avarice and greed," said Judge Joseph G. McIntyre. Olah, convicted of sixteen counts of helping doctors, a lawyer, a Weyburn city administrator, and businessmen avoid paying taxes, was considered the principal conspirator.

On appeal, Olah's lawyer pleaded for leniency. "Olah suffered the most as a result of the case. The others are doctors and a pharmacist and after having served their sentences, they will carry on with their professions. But Olah has been finished since 1975 as an art dealer." The appeal failed, and Olah went off to jail to serve two years less a day.

A decade later, a new, aspiring artist was filling his diner in downtown Regina with his paintings. Roger Ing, the eclectic owner of the New Utopia Café, called his work "Rogerisms."

With its brilliant colours, free style, and erratic form, Rogerism reminded one man of the surrealism and abstract impressionism of the noted Canadian artist Jean-Paul Riopelle. But while a Rogerism could be had for a few dollars, a Riopelle commanded thousands. The astute buyer bought several. He knew the works had potential.

He also commissioned work—paying another fledgling artist to reproduce paintings from books.

Contrary to his lawyer's prediction, Joseph Olah Jr. was back in business.

In December 1991, an auction house situated across the

street from the Regina police station was getting ready to put two dozen paintings and prints on the block. The listing included "Portrait of Lady" by James Henderson. There was also "Mountains at Banff" by Illingworth Kerr and "Trees by River" by Saskatoon artist Dorothy Knowles. A drawing attributed to the Group of Seven's A.Y. Jackson was expected to garner a lot of interest. And it did attract interest—from the police. Half the paintings were forgeries. The person who had put them in the sale had been duped when he originally bought them.

For eleven years, restaurateurs, a lawyer, a realtor and other shrewd investors had been buying up fine works of art from a man they trusted. Some had so much faith in the bright, manipulative art dealer, they bought his paintings even while he was on parole from his previous crime.

A long-time friend of Olah's, who had testified in his defence in 1978, could not believe his good fortune when he paid $2,400 for a half-interest in what was supposed to be the work of Canadian artist Jack Bush. Olah assured him it would sell for $60,000. While waiting for documents authenticating the painting, the friend did some research and noted it was not in the artist's usual style. But Olah assured him the unusual style made it even more rare and valuable. The same buyer invested $1,000 for a one-third share in a Riopelle, told it would make $20,000. Both were actually "Rogerisms," worth about twenty bucks a piece.

The charismatic, enigmatic Olah said the paintings he sold were by such Canadian talents as Emily Carr, James Henderson, Ernest Lindner, and Allen Sapp. Six willing buyers believed him, shelling out $15,540 for what they believed was a bargain.

A master in the art of deception, Olah was sent back to jail.

Sour Milk

THE LAST TIME GERTIE SCHILL SAW HER HUSBAND HERB, HE was heading out the door to go milk the cows. It was a Sunday. He and their eldest child, 7-year-old Theresa, had gone to church that morning in Lebret with Herb's cousin. Heavy with their fifth child, Gertie stayed back at the farm with their three youngest. Herb took a nap later that afternoon before getting ready to do the chores. He pulled his denim overalls up over the trousers he had worn when he and Gertie married eight years earlier. They were held up by his "wedding belt," the buckle bearing an H.

When she saw Herb again, eight months later, his decomposed body was lying at Stiff's Undertaking Parlours at Fort San. There was little left of the man she had known. But Gertie had no doubt it was him. She recognized the wedding pants. The matching suit coat and vest were at home. Gertie knew him by his worn felt hat and the glasses he had just started wearing about a month before he went missing. She recognized his silver pocket watch, the hands stopped at fifteen minutes after nine. Its face was stamped with the unmistakable diamond and letter E trademark of Eaton's. There was a chip opposite the numeral ten. It had been that way when Herb got the watch in a trade with his brother Bill. It was a year before his disappearance. Twenty years earlier, the watch was Bill's birthday present from their father. Now in death, it was one of the few personal items that revealed the identity of Gertie's 33-year-old husband.

Herbert Schill had been found that chilly, damp morning by neighbours digging in the manure pile behind the barn on the couple's farm. It was three miles north of Lebret in the picturesque Qu'Appelle Valley. The men had been digging for about an hour and a half when Joseph Mlazgar and Paul Bedel hit something brittle with their five-tine pitchforks. They tossed two more forkfuls of rotting dung and straw aside to reveal a skull. It still sported Herb's long, black strands of hair. Buried four feet under and fifteen feet in from the edge of the pile, Herb—or what remained of him—was lying on his right side with his knees slightly bent. His clothing had kept the bones and bits of decayed tissue together. Aside from the watch, the farmer's pockets still held his jackknife, a bit of wire and staples, his pipe and tobacco pouch, and three handkerchiefs.

WHEN HERB DIDN'T COME HOME on October 16, 1938, Gertie initially thought he had been delayed, maybe helping a neighbour with an injured horse. He and their hired man Stanley Illerbrun, the cousin who had joined Herb at church that morning, had gone to milk the cows. An hour later, Stanley alone returned with the milk and one empty pail. He told Gertie he saw lights shining in the barn and heard a car pull into the yard. A man had come to the barn door and called for Herb, who left with the stranger while Stanley finished milking the cows. Stanley even found tire tracks in the farmyard. There was still no sign of Herb the next morning. Gertie called police that night at Stanley's urging. Tracking dogs searched—to no avail.

Herb's 34th birthday passed that November without him, as did the birth of his last child that same month. Stanley remained at the farm to help out Gertie, until she left just before Christmas to spend the winter in

Kamloops, BC, with her mother. Gertie noticed after Herb vanished that she could never catch Stanley's eyes when she spoke to him. He always looked away. Then when he thought she wasn't looking, he would watch her. Stanley no longer wanted to go out to the barn alone after dark.

He had worked for his cousin for the past two years. His family had their own farm near Illerbrun, the town named for his father. But drought and dust storms had hit the southwest particularly hard, and they had not had a crop to speak of in a decade. The family of eight was getting government relief, but the money didn't stretch far enough.

Stanley, being the eldest son, went to work for his cousin. The first year, he sent home $100 to his ailing father. Stanley and Herb seemed to get along well, for the most part. There was one time, about a month or so before Herb disappeared, when he had reprimanded the muscular, dark-haired, good-looking hired man for going into the bedroom of the young woman who was helping during threshing. Herb said not to let it happen again, and Stanley seemed content.

Rumours abounded about the missing farmer. Originally from the States, Herb had lived in the area almost all his life and was not known to have any enemies. There was speculation about a gang from North Dakota, or that he had run out on his wife and five children. Some wondered if he hadn't drowned in the nearby lake. RCMP spoke again to Gertie in the spring. She remembered how Herb and Stanley had once buried a colt in the manure pile to decompose.

Searchers returned to the Schill farm. After Herb's body was unearthed on June 7, 1939, the Mounties paid Stanley a visit.

The 19-year-old admitted he had not been getting along with his boss. Stanley complained that Herb wanted to cut his wages. He still owed him $90. "I was supposed to get two Sundays a month off, and for two months I never had any," he said.

They went out to milk the seven cows. Herb took one pail, and Stanley the other. Two of the animals were going dry. "He had two pretty hard cows, and I always had to milk these. So I got sore and told him I wasn't going to milk them," Stanley said.

The mood soured.

Each man stepped away from his cow. "What are you trying to pull off anyhow?" Herb asked. The argument spilled onto the barn floor. Herb hit his cousin in the shoulder. Stanley tried to swing back, but missed. Herb again cuffed his cousin, who responded with a jab. Emotions frothed.

At trial, Stanley's confession changed slightly. He said Herb had come after him with his pitchfork. "He told me that he would let my guts out if I did not quit."

Stanley said he was looking for a pitchfork when he spotted Herb's .22-rifle hanging by its trigger on a nail in the cow barn. As essential a farm tool as a shovel or a hoe, the gun was kept handy to deal with nuisance skunks.

Stanley jumped through a two-foot-wide hole into the adjoining horse barn. He fished in his pocket and came up with a shell, loaded, and fired once over the backs of the cows. He told the jury he intended only to frighten Herb. But the shot found the back of his cousin's head.

Stanley knew he was in deep trouble.

He dug himself in deeper.

Grabbing hold of Herb—160 pounds—Stanley dragged him 400 feet to the manure pile. After the crude burial, the hired man thought up a story while he finished milking the last four cows himself.

He was working again on a Sunday.

Except Stanley did not milk the two tough cows.

Author's note: Stanley Illerbrun was twice tried for murder in the death of his cousin. Despite his pleas that he never intended to kill Herbert Schill, Illerbrun was twice convicted of murder. He was hanged in Regina on June 21, 1940.

Dr. John and Mr. Schneeberger

THE VANITY LICENCE PLATE READ SIMPLY **SCHNEE**. FOR Larry O'Brien, the six letters meant opportunity. The car door was unlocked. Pulling open the ashtray, O'Brien spotted a small black and white tube of lip balm. It had been used. Private investigator O'Brien pulled out an envelope and smeared the tip of the balm onto the plastic window. He put that envelope into another. Inside the envelope, inside the balm, the saliva and skin cells were trapped.

By that time, Katie had been waiting four years for justice. And she was not known for her patience.

The quick-tempered woman had once slugged her boyfriend during an argument at a fundraiser for the local swimming pool in Kipling. Dr. John Schneeberger was at the same event and knew from seeing the fight that Katie was not a woman to be crossed.

THE RESPECTED, WELL-LIKED Dr. John—as most people called him—had spearheaded efforts to get the pool built. He wasn't from this small rural town. He wasn't even from Canada. But the 31-year-old South African transplant had become one of Kipling's favourite sons since opening his practice in December 1988. He was credited with saving heart patients. He introduced a sex education course to the high school. Dr. John chaired the board of a workshop for disabled adults. Twice he had intervened on behalf of men in trouble with the law and convinced a minister to accept them into his home to spare them from a jail cell. While Dr. John won praise at the fundraiser that summer evening in 1992, Katie fuelled gossip with her outburst.

Her anger reached a flashpoint again a few months later when her now former boyfriend drove into the gas station where Katie was working on Halloween night. He had asked another woman out for supper. Katie, who had thought she and her ex might still reconcile, dented the driver's door on his pick-up truck with her kick. He fled the parking lot, but his departure did little to change her mood. Katie left work early to find her friend working at the hospital. As it turned out, the woman wasn't on shift. But a nurse offered to call a doctor for the distraught Katie.

Dr. John caught the first few minutes of the popular television show *L.A. Law* before heading out to the hospital. By chance, he was the doctor on call that night. But he knew Katie anyway. The 24-year-old single mother had been his patient for about a year. Nine months earlier, he had delivered her daughter in the same hospital where she now sat crying and upset.

Katie was in an examination room when Dr. John walked in. The dark-haired doctor with the boyish good looks promised something to help calm her nerves. Katie trusted Dr. John when he injected a liquid into the vein of her right arm. It would help her relax, he assured her with his soft, comforting accent. She felt dizzy and limp as the quick-acting sedative took effect. The doctor came to her side, helping her lie in a fetal position on the examining table. Dr. John was always so compassionate, so caring.

Suddenly, there was the unexpected tugging at her jeans, and her panties were pushed to one side. Katie's body was numb, but her mind alert. As she lay facing the wall, she felt a penis rubbing against her. Then he was inside her. Katie could not move. She could not scream.

She could not do anything. She had no choice but to lay there. The young woman looking for help had been immobilized by a drug used to still patients undergoing surgery. The powerful anaesthetic Versed can also cause amnesia.

Schneeberger knew all about Versed and its effects. During his studies in South Africa, he had won an award for being the best final-year student in anaesthesiology.

Katie willed her right arm to move. It responded ever so slightly. But it was enough. The assault on her body stopped. Her pants were quickly cinched back up. Katie lay there stunned as the physician who had taken an oath to do no harm casually took his coat off the door knob and walked out.

She was confused. Perhaps her mind was playing tricks. But the zipper was halfway open on her pants, and she could feel her wet underwear off to one side.

Katie knew something had happened in that examining room.

"What was the drug that you gave me last night?" Katie confronted her doctor as he discharged her from the hospital the next day.

"Why? Did you have wild dreams?" Schneeberger scoffed. "It wasn't a dream," Katie shot back.

When she got home, Katie sealed her panties in a plastic bag. She knew the rapist had left his genetic fingerprint. The DNA in his semen would prove her right—just like the samples taken for the rape kit when Katie was examined the next day at a Regina hospital.

Then she waited.

Two weeks later, an RCMP officer collected a blood sample from Dr. John. A lab technician had started to draw the blood, when the doctor intervened. Taking the needle, Dr. John inserted it into his own arm, just above the elbow. When the Mountie noticed the doctor's upper arm was bruised, Dr. John blamed it on a lab technician hitting a tendon during an earlier test. The Mountie left with two vials, satisfied with the doctor's explanation.

Katie was furious when the officer called with the results. The DNA contained in Dr. John's blood had not come from the same man who left his semen on Katie's underwear and body. "That's impossible," she said, confronting the Mountie. In this two-doctor town, the officer was another of Dr. John's patients. Katie grew suspicious.

The rumours had started almost immediately in the town of 1,100 people. And Dr. John, who had since been appointed the chief of medical staff, was winning the war of words. But even if no one else wanted to believe her, Katie knew Schneeberger was a rapist. Nearly a year would pass before she'd get a second chance to prove it.

This time, the senior officer in charge of the local detachment went to get the blood samples. Frustrated with the lab technician's attempt to find a vein, Dr. John once again took hold of the needle himself. Barely a centimetre of brownish blood trickled into each of the two vials.

Once again, DNA tests showed the blood taken from Dr. John's arm and the semen left on Katie's panties had come from different people. RCMP closed the case file.

Dr. John's reputation grew; Katie's had been destroyed. She moved away from her hometown.

Her simmering anger reached a boil. Convinced she couldn't trust the local police, Katie borrowed money from her parents to sue the doctor and hired her own private investigator. On March 23, 1996, Larry O'Brien, a former Mountie, found the lip balm in Schneeberger's car. Sent off to a private lab for DNA testing, the results were startling. The genetic material on the lip balm matched the semen stains. It didn't match the blood drawn from Schneeberger's own arm.

At Katie's insistence, there was a third test in November 1996. Four years after providing the first blood sample, Schneeberger sat in the RCMP crime lab in Regina with a videotape camera recording the event. He insisted the blood be taken from his arm instead of the usual finger prick. The near miniscule amount of liquid drawn looked dark, almost black. Like the blood taken from a corpse. The sample was so degraded, no testing could be done.

In the spring of 1997, Katie heard that a second patient had made a complaint.

THE ATHLETIC 15-YEAR-OLD said the doctor had put his hands on her naked body a number of times beginning when she was 13. And it was not for a medical exam. He had put his fingers into her body, and asked the frightened teen about orgasms. He had also given her injections. Saline to flush her veins, he told her. Usually, Sue could not remember anything after the injections. But once while lying on an examining table at his clinic after she had become dizzy, she heard a snapping sound. Like a condom. Later, she could smell lubricant on her panties. There was another needle when she had a wart removed. Sue again didn't know what had happened. But she had her suspicions, especially when she found a condom wrapper.

Now, with the second patient's allegations against Dr. John, his wife and mother of their two young daughters went from ally to adversary. She turned over boxes of condoms, needles and drugs found in the home they'd built together. Among her husband's stash of medical supplies was the potent sedative Versed.

In December 1997, an officer showed up at Dr. John's office and plucked two dozen hairs from his head. The DNA gleaned from the hair was a genetic match for the semen from Katie's panties. But, perhaps more surprisingly, the hair from the doctor's head didn't match the blood that supposedly flowed through his veins during the earlier tests.

Two weeks after Dr. John saw Katie in the examining room in 1992, he had treated Danny Szabo for a stomach ailment. The doctor had drawn Danny's blood. Knowing he was due to give the RCMP a blood sample, Schneeberger had taken a bit extra and put it in a fridge in his clinic. The blood drawn from the doctor's arm matched Danny's genetic profile perfectly. His blood was in Schneeberger's arm.

By the time the doctor went on trial, seven years had passed since Katie was a patient at his mercy. Time had not worn her down. When Schneeberger's experienced lawyer grilled her about the sensation on her skin in the examining room, her temper flared once more. "We'll drug you on Versed, and you can explain to us how it feels," she fired back.

This time, it was not Katie who had most people talking; it was the brazen doctor. The man proclaiming his innocence told how he had put Szabo's blood into his arm to trick three genetic tests. When the RCMP requested the first test, the skilled doctor grasped a scalpel in his right hand and cut open his upper left arm. Into the wound, he pushed a fifteen-centimetre long rubber tube normally used as a drain in surgical procedures. The sausage-like tube, a centimetre in diameter, was filled with Szabo's blood. After the test, Schneeberger took the tube out and bandaged his arm.

Nine months later, he did it again, reopening the wound and reinserting the tube of Szabo's blood for the second test.

Certain there might be more demands for blood tests after hearing Katie had hired a private eye, Schneeberger put the tube back into his bicep in April 1996 and left it there. When the third blood test was done more than seven months later, it yielded the old, blackened blood.

Schneeberger served nearly all of his six-year sentence in prison for sexually assaulting Katie and Sue, giving Katie an overpowering drug to commit the sexual assault, and obstructing justice by providing false blood samples. When the sentence expired, he was deported back to South Africa despite his efforts to remain in Canada, near his now ex-wife and two daughters. There is a good chance he would have stayed—but for getting caught by his own lies. His Canadian citizenship was revoked because he did not tell the truth in February 1993 when asked if he was currently or ever had been under a criminal investigation.

Such deception. Such betrayal. Yet some still refused to believe Dr. John had raped a vulnerable, drugged patient on Halloween night, or a teenager in his care.

"The Dr. Schneeberger I knew was a man who cared deeply for human beings," a letter reads. "I cannot see him as an evil man." It was written by one of ten people who sent letters to Justice Ellen Gunn, pleading for their beloved Dr. John, even after she had found him guilty of four crimes.

"I am sending this letter to you in hope that it may help the judge see another side of John Schneeberger," wrote another former patient in praise of the fine physician.

But clearly, the judge had been convinced there was another side to this doctor.

Katie and Sue are pseudonyms. A publication ban ordered by the judge prohibits disclosing any information which could identify them.

Copycat

THE PIMPLY-FACED TEEN WITH THE THIN GOATEE LIFTS HIS shaved head from the bunk bed, turns and gives his new cell-mate a nod.

Keith Pearce, his long hair held back in a braid, tips his head in response and sighs anxiously as he takes a spot on one of the four bunks lining the small cell in the Swift Current RCMP detachment.

"Welcome to Saskatchewan," Leroy Michael Linn says. The 18-year-old from Powell River, BC, had earlier overheard Pearce tell one of the RCMP officers he was from Edmonton. The inmates chuckle at their predicament.

Pearce confides that he had been on his way to Regina before his buddy got him arrested with about a half-pound of coke and $30,000 worth of steroids.

"No shit?" says Linn.

"Yeah," Pearce replies.

"I got arrested in Kyle in a truck with no insurance," Linn says. "It wasn't my truck," he adds with a laugh.

"I hear ya,'" says Pearce. "Say no more."

It was probably good advice. But Linn was warming up to this stranger. "Did you come through Kyle?" he asks.

His cell-mate seems uncertain. "There was a town I figured we'd got some heat," says Pearce.

Linn smiles. "Did you see yellow tape around a gas station and a bunch of cops?"

"Yeah, that's right," Pearce replies, but he cannot recall what station specifically. Linn quickly fills in the blank. Esso.

Shifting from his prone position on the bunk, Linn points at himself with his right thumb. He forms his thumb and forefinger into a gun and fires into the air. Then, he raises his fore and middle fingers to indicate two, and smiles.

"Really, eh?" says Pearce, recalling a radio report about a double murder in Kyle.

"I did it," brags Linn. "That was me." It happened around eight o'clock the night before.

"I walked in while my buddy waited in the truck," Linn says. "Got $540 from it, though."

"Good score!" Pearce says, encouraging his new friend to continue talking.

Linn agrees. "The cops still haven't found the gun I used. Man, I was sorry to lose that one ... I used a .357 Magnum Smith and Wesson with a six-inch barrel. It was a blue cobalt colour," he adds. Linn had stolen it from his father before heading down the highway. He takes pride in what a good shot he is, how on a quick draw he can hit the bull's-eye of a target from twenty-five yards.

"My buddy didn't know what I was going to do. But I had it all planned," Linn says. "There were two women ... I even got a full tank of gas. She pumped it for me."

"I took some cigarettes and some munchies," Linn continues. "And then I pulled out my gun. I said, 'Give me the money, you know, from the till.' ... She says 'No.'"

"Then I said, 'No? Really? Well, fuck you.' And I shot her in the chest." Linn demonstrates by holding his right arm straight out, simulating a gun held sideways, and Pearce is struck by how the move resembles actor Brad Pitt in the movie *Kalifornia*.

Linn continues with his chilling monologue: "Then I

Stanley Illerbrun, 1939. © Department of Justice. Reproduced with the permission of the Minister of Public Works and Government Services Canada (2007). Source: Library and Archives Canada/ Department of Justice fonds/RG13-B-1/Volume 1623, part 1, file no. cc 506. See "Sour Milk."

Sandy Charles, photographer Richard Marjan, courtesy *Saskatoon StarPhoenix*, June 19, 1996. See "The Boy Who Wanted To Fly."

Left: Kim Friebus (photographer unknown), courtesy *Saskatoon StarPhoenix*, June 21, 1991. See "Brown Fall."
Right: John Schneeberger, photographer Don Healy, courtesy *Regina Leader-Post*, September 23, 1999. See: "Dr. John and Mr. Schneeberger."

Leroy Linn, photographer Trevor Suttor, courtesy Regina Leader-Post, October 20, 1998. See "Copycat."

Left: Steven Kummerfeld (foreground) and Alex Ternowetsky (background), photographer Bryan Schlosser, courtesy *Regina Leader-Post*, November 12, 1996. See "Worlds Apart."

Right: John Crawford, photographer Bryan Schlosser, courtesy *Regina Leader-Post*, January 21, 1999. See "The Hunter and the Hunted."

Dawn Kickley, photographer Trevor Sutter, courtesy *Regina Leader-Post*, June 11, 1990. See "The Mayor's Daughter."

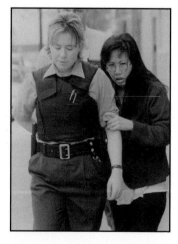

Left: Robert Kieling, photographer Bryan Schlosser, courtesy *Regina Leader-Post*, January 15, 1985. See "An Area of Insanity."
Right: Lana Nguyen, photographer Don Healy, courtesy *Regina Leader-Post*, May 15, 2001. See "The Power of Persuasion."

Carney Nerland (left) at Alberta Aryan Fest, a white supremacist gathering on an acreage outside Prevost, Alberta, courtesy CTV Calgary 1990. See "The Truth About Carney."

Left: James (Max) Yanoshewski, photographer Bob Watson, courtesy *Regina Leader-Post*, September 29, 1994. See "Of Death and Survival." Right: Stuart Neubauer, photographer Bob Jamieson, courtesy *Regina Leader-Post*, January 13, 1987. See "Grocery Misconduct."

Painting purportedly by Canaletto entered as exhibit at Joseph Olah Jr. trial, courtesy *Regina Leader-Post*, May 4, 1978. See "Art and Avarice."

Left: Nick Bonamy, photographer Richard Marjan, courtesy *Saskatoon StarPhoenix*, May 15, 2006. See "Gold Watches and White Collars."
Right: Serena Nicotine, photographer Richard Marjan, courtesy *Saskatoon StarPhoenix*, March 8, 1999. See "No Place for Serenity."

David Hares (left) and Robert Gulash (right), photographer Patrick Petit, courtesy *Regina Leader-Post*, November 2, 1976. See "Football, Fowl Suppers, and Funerals."

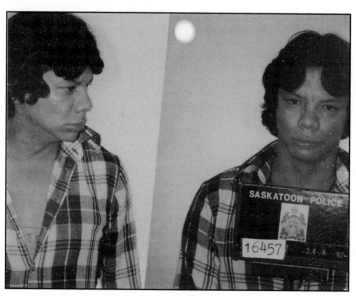

Robert Ironchild, Saskatoon City Police photo. See "Whiter Than Mine."

Gary Gillingwater, photographer Bryan Schlosser, courtesy *Regina Leader-Post*, June 28, 2001. See "Top Dog."

Left: Ziadten Boughanmi, photographer Bryan Schlosser, courtesy *Regina Leader-Post*, October 10, 1990. See "In His Mind."
Right: Larry Clare Deckert, photographer Don Healy, courtesy *Regina Leader-Post*. See "Unforgotten."

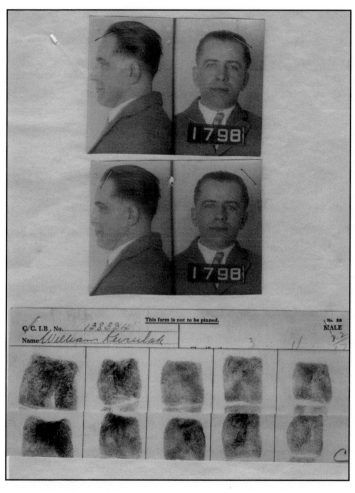

Photo and fingerprints: William Kurulak, 1932. © Department of Justice. Reproduced with the permission of the Minister of Public Works and Government Services Canada (2007). Source: Library and Archives Canada/ Department of Justice fonds/RG-13-B-1/Volume 1576, file no. cc 376. See "The Painting."

Photo: Alex Oshuk, 1928. © Department of Justice. Reproduced with the permission of the Minister of Public Works and Government Services Canada (2007). Source: Library and Archives Canada/ Department of Justice fonds/RG13-B-1/File no. cc 272. See "The Darkness of the Night."

A page from John "Al" Lyon's scrapbook. At top left, David Thurston Brown is pictured being fingerprinted by law enforcement officials in Montana. Sgt. Lyon appears with Montana law enforcement, and alone at bottom right. Scrapboook courtesy Al Lyon's family. See "The Long Ride."

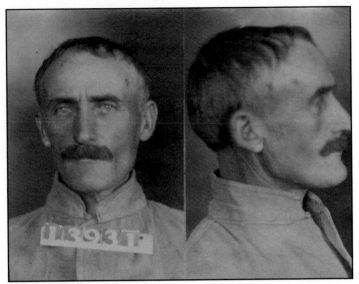

Photo: Valentine Schmidt, 1927. © Department of Justice. Reproduced with the permission of the Minister of Public Works and Government Services Canada (2007). Source: Library and Archives Canada/ Department of Justice fonds/RG13-B-1/Volume 1544, file no. cc 263. See "Spotless to the End."

Nathan Oxby, photographer Roy Antal, courtesy *Regina Leader-Post*, October 25, 2000. See "It Would Explode the Heart."

turned to the other woman and told her to get the money. She refused too. So I shot her in the head. Then I went around to the till. I shot the first woman in the head."

"What a haul for a small town!" he says.

"I'd say so," Pearce replies. He is clearly a man of few words.

"Yeah," Linn says. "Three shots—one in the chest and two in the head."

Linn ran back to the truck where his buddy, wondering what had happened, was waiting. "Shut up or I'll shoot you next," said the two-time killer.

Linn picks up his story, telling Pearce how they sped out of Kyle stopping only by a slough where he hurled his weapon, hoping the cobalt-blue would become one with the water. His tale ends with his capture at a roadblock northwest of Kyle, about two and a half hours after the shootings.

In the glow cast by headlights and roadside flares, a lone officer at a highway junction saw a figure walking towards him with his hands in the air. Corporal Matt Lowther at first mistook him for a friend, until the man said, "I'm the one you're looking for. I did the armed robbery and shot that lady."

Linn then added, "I didn't mean to shoot her."

The officer did not take his hands off his service revolver until his prisoner was handcuffed.

As Linn's conversation with his new-found buddy in the Swift Current cell reaches a lull, he punctuates his story with one more detail. "I'm a natural-born killer," he says, hoping to impress his guest. "What a rush!"

There was only one problem with all this bravado. Pearce was not a drug courier from Edmonton. He was a Mountie—and he'd just got his man.

The 36-year-old Alberta RCMP officer who specialized in undercover work had indeed heard about Linn's deeds from a radio report. At the time, Pearce was inside the cab of a tractor, using his vacation time in Gravelbourg to help out family with spring seeding. He telephoned the under-cover co-ordinator in Saskatchewan and offered his expertise. Almost twenty-six hours later, he was sharing a cell with Linn, a self-described natural-born killer. Sandra Veason and Diane McLaren lost their lives in a community of 500 where peace and safety were taken for granted until that day.

In the 1994 movie *Natural Born Killers*, Woody Harrelson and Juliette Lewis go on a bloody rampage of robbery and murder in small-town USA. *Natural Born Killers* was Linn's favourite. He also owned a copy of *Kalifornia*, another movie about a killing spree. Was Linn a psychopath drawn to such films? Or was it *Natural Born Killers* and *Kalifornia* that inspired him to commit the horrible acts that occurred at Kyle's Rebco Esso on May 6, 1997—midway into Diane McLaren's four-hour shift?

Diane, who planned to soon open a greenhouse business, had been working part-time at the service station to make a bit of extra money so her four children could pursue post-secondary schooling. The 44-year-old had been eagerly awaiting her son's graduation in June and her elder son's wedding a month later. Diane had met her husband exactly twenty-five years to the day she encountered Linn.

Sandra shared her friend's passion for flowers and lived across the street from the station. On what would turn out to be the last day of her life, she had dropped by for a visit and a coffee. A married mother with an adult son, 54-year-old Sandra had recently become a grandmother at the time of her death.

Linn would be convicted by a jury of second-degree murder and given a life sentence without parole eligibility for twenty-two years. A mental health worker who had known him as a teen described Linn as a sad and lonely boy who suffered from rages, panic attacks, and depression. At his sentencing, the man who had spoken so bluntly, so callously in his jail cell about taking two lives was suddenly at a loss for words.

"Everybody knows how this happened, and the question is, 'Why?'" Linn said. "I wish I could answer that question, but I do not know that answer myself."

Dining With Daniel

DANIEL BENKOVIC IS A MAN WHO APPRECIATES THE FINER things in life.

He particularly likes to sit down and have a nice meal, toss back a few drinks and enjoy the evening. He never has any trouble finding people to join him for dinner; Benkovic is funny and outgoing, and people like him.

When dining with friends Benkovic usually picks up the tab, generously insisting everything is put on his bill so his guests can enjoy the night without worrying about the cost. Like that time at the nice pasta place downtown.

It was a big group, and they racked up quite a bill. Hundreds of dollars, but Daniel didn't mind.

He wasn't going to pay it anyway.

He got away with that one, but it didn't really matter. He would find himself standing in the prisoner's dock at Regina Provincial Court again soon enough, facing the familiar charge. He knows it by heart: Section 364 in the Criminal Code of Canada. Fraudulently obtaining food.

On a February day in 2000, Benkovic has well over 100 previous convictions on his record, and that doesn't even count the ones he never got caught for. There are a lot of those, too.

Since the 1980s, most of Benkovic's convictions are for

food fraud. "Dining and dashing" as it is commonly known.

Benkovic tells the judge his alcoholism is responsible for much of his trouble.

"I'd been drinking off and on," he says. "Well, mostly on."

Born in Yugoslavia in 1957, Benkovic came to Canada as a child with his mother, stepfather and younger brother, and the family settled in Regina. Benkovic was incarcerated for the first time at 16, and has been in and out of jail ever since. He's spent most of his life behind bars—all for minor offenses.

Certainly, Benkovic has problems. He's diagnosed as having Bipolar Disorder with Hypomanic Episodes and is an alcoholic. Medication helps control his manic episodes, but Benkovic stops taking his medication if he's planning to drink.

He's well known to the judges, lawyers and staff at Regina Provincial Court — and to those in the restaurant industry. His court documents read like an executive's expense account: Regent Family restaurant $114; Orleans Café and Oyster Bar $25.07; Brass Lantern $51.93; Trifon's Pizza $70.85; The Keg $70; Viet Thay $33.64.

"You're a menace to anyone who runs a restaurant in this city," Judge Kenn Bellerose told Benkovic in 2002, while sentencing him to five months in jail. "How do we stop you? What deters you?"

Bellerose was further dismayed to see that some of the new offences took place the same day he released Benkovic from custody weeks earlier. The judge had been swayed by Benkovic's newfound religious conviction.

"I released you because you found God, but by 4:15 you had found another restaurant," Bellerose said.

A contrite Benkovic suggested some time in jail would be an appropriate punishment.

"Jail's probably the best thing for me...," he told the judge. "A roof over my heard, three squares a day. I'm getting burned out."

But five years later, Benkovic is still in the same court-house, before the same judges, facing the same charges. The only thing that's changed is the number of convictions.

Waiting to be sentenced on some new food frauds in 2007, Benkovic relaxes in an upstairs courtroom. He's wearing a crisp black T-shirt from the Rolling Stones concert in Regina—the famous tongue waggling with a Saskatchewan flag—under a suit jacket. His hair is a mop of curls, his face friendly and animated.

Benkovic says he's thought of taking his "food fraud thing" to other cities—there are a lot of good restaraunts out there, after all—and at least people wouldn't know him. Not like in Regina, where the restaurant industry circulates his picture.

He's never left the city, though. He says every time he's ready to go he gets arrested on new charges.

What to do with the chronic dine-and-dasher continues to eat at the judges he appears before, and Benkovic's credit may be running short.

Benkovic says his behaviour is a compulsion, much like gambling or shoplifting, and that his mental illness and overwhelming urge for alcohol fuel his deceptive dining.

But with a sly wink and a mischievous grin, he also admits he gets a charge out of it.

"I'm on a high when I do these things," he confided to a parole officer once. "It's a feeling of power, wealth. In my own mind I have the money."

The Truth About Carney

His name was Carney, but his friends called him Milt. Sometimes he also went by Kurt Meyer, a name he borrowed from a Nazi general who executed twenty Saskatchewan soldiers during the Second World War. But whatever you called him, Carney Nerland was a racist. He had been for a long time.

As a junior high school student in Prince Albert, Nerland was a bully who dressed in German military style, disrupted classes with racist jokes, and spent his free time reading about the Nazi movement and collecting Nazi memorabilia. He once referred to Adolf Hitler as "a prophet set forth by God in the last days" and said the Holocaust was "the biggest misshapen misrepresented sickish joke of the 20th century."

It was a natural fit when Nerland joined the Ku Klux Klan in 1984, in his late teens, and that same year became a member of the Church of Jesus Christ Christian-Aryan Nations, a fervent white supremacist group based inside a guarded Idaho compound. Among other things, the group advocated killing minorities and Jews for points, toward the goal of attaining the ultimate status of Aryan Warrior.

As his involvement with the organizations grew, Nerland spent a weekend with KKK leader David Duke in

Louisiana, and headed a Saskatchewan branch of the Aryan "church." He was becoming a prominent figure in Canada's white supremacist movement.

Late in the summer of 1990, Nerland was front and centre at the Albertan Aryan Fest, a white supremacist gathering held on an acreage outside Provost. Nerland handled security for the meeting, and spent the weekend stalking through the grounds in military clothing and a swastika armband.

When protestors gathered outside the gate, a gun-toting Nerland confronted a man dressed in a concentration camp uniform and dared the man to approach.

"You survived Auschwitz, you'll survive me," Nerland taunted.

As the TV cameras rolled, Nerland's tirade against the man continued.

"You're one of the ones they didn't work to death, you parasite. You fucking weren't able to work in the camps good enough to feed the Nazi war machine," he said. "What the fuck are you doing over here you piece of shit? You lying son of a bitch."

Nerland told the man a gas chamber was being made that day, and promised "If you stay around long enough and you cross this line, we'll put you in it."

Then Nerland walked to the gate and pumped his shotgun for the reporters and protestors outside the fence.

"This is called Native birth control," he said. "A 12-gauge cuts a person right in half, it's just great for preventing further births."

Six months later, Nerland shot a Native man in the back.

Leo LaChance was a farmhand and trapper from the Big River Reserve who had grown up poor and lived hard. At 48, he dulled the pain of his life by drinking Lysol and Listerine, and eked out a meagre existence on the reserve. But despite his problems, LaChance was always kind and polite to others, rarely cursed or used harsh language, and was described by one police officer as the type of man who wouldn't hurt a fly. His friends and family said he was good-natured and liked to joke around and laugh.

On the evening of January 28, 1991, LaChance loaded up a bag of fur pelts and caught a ride from the reserve into Prince Albert. He headed to the Katz Fur Shop, where he had sold his wares in the past. The store was closed, so LaChance dropped his bag of furs outside and went into the store next door, the Northern Pawn and Gun Shop. Nerland, the gun shop's co-owner, was drinking rye and Coke and talking about the Gulf War with two friends when LaChance walked in.

Their meeting was brief.

LaChance left the store a moment later, picked up his bag of furs and walked a short distance before collapsing onto the ground.

Kim Koroll, a city of Prince Albert engineer, was driving by when he saw LaChance fall face-first onto the sidewalk. Koroll stopped and, seeing that something was seriously wrong with LaChance, went into the Northern Pawn and Gun Shop to call 9-1-1.

Koroll said there was an injured man lying outside on the sidewalk, and asked to use the phone to call an ambulance. Nerland said no, so Koroll called 9-1-1 from a fast food restaurant across the street.

As his life drained away, LaChance tried to speak, but much of what he said was in Cree and could not be understood by police and medical staff. In hospital he told police he had tried to sell his furs to three white men, but they didn't want them. He told police there was no argument and he didn't know why he had been shot in the back.

It must have been an accident, he said.

He died in hospital a short time later.

NERLAND WAS DOING SOME TALKING TOO.

"If I shot that Indian, I'm fucked," he told his friends after the shooting. "My business is fucked."

One of his friends, an employee of the Ministry of Social Services, had other worries.

"You silly bugger," he said. "You could have hit my car."

The next day Nerland was arrested in Alberta and charged with manslaughter.

As Nerland's case moved through the courts, his racial views continued to surface. Appearing in court for a bail hearing, Nerland told a police constable he'd only eat food prepared by a white man.

"I'm not eating any gook food made by a Chinaman. I'd starve first," he said. "I need to lose weight anyway."

Returning to the jail later that day, he told the constable he should get a medal for killing an Indian. "I've done you all a favour," he said.

On April 11, just less than three months after the shooting, Nerland pleaded guilty to manslaughter. His lawyer, Earl Kalenith, said LaChance's death was completely unintentional.

"There was nothing relating to race involved in this accident," Kalenith said. "It was plain and simple an accident, albeit one which resulted from the dangerous use of a firearm."

Nerland echoed his lawyer's claims.

"I do regret the tragic loss of life," he told the court. "It was my own irresponsibility and dangerous use of a firearm and I accept my responsibility."

Based on a joint recommendation by his lawyer and the Crown, Nerland was sentenced to four years in prison. The sentence didn't sit well with many people, nor did Nerland's story. How could an experienced shooter, the owner of a gun shop, be careless enough to accidentally shoot someone? Why didn't he check to see whether LaChance had been hit? How could the unprovoked shooting of an Aboriginal man by a well-known white supremacist not be racially motivated?

"Saying the death was not racially motivated is an

insult to my intelligence," said the leader of one Prince Albert First Nations organization.

In the midst of the uproar, a public inquiry was struck to take another look at the case.

Nerland initially refused to take part in the inquiry, and co-operated only after being charged with contempt of court. Fearing violence from both Aboriginals and white supremacists, Nerland appeared to testify under heavy security.

He was different—or at least he looked different—nearly unrecognizable after having lost at least 100 pounds. Some saw a change in attitude, too. He was attempting to be earnest and polite, not as brash and belligerent as he'd been in the past.

Nerland told the inquiry he hadn't been a white supremacist since 1985, and that everything since then was simply play-acting. He denied many of the racist statements attributed to him, and described his televised comment about Native birth control as merely "an untoward joke."

He said he remembered little of the night of the shooting, and didn't even recall LaChance coming into the store.

"I know it was an accident," he said. "There was no intent whatsoever."

The inquiry's three commissioners released their report in November 1993, just weeks before Nerland was released from prison and into the witness protection program after serving two-thirds of his sentence.

The commissioners found there were mistakes in the investigation, including failing to consider racism as a possible motive—a consideration which could have made the difference between manslaughter and murder. The Crown laid the right charge with the information it had, the commissioners decided, but police and prosecutors should have investigated the shooting more thoroughly.

Lingering questions about whether Nerland was working as a paid RCMP informant on white supremacist activity, as some media reported, and whether that played a part in how his case was handled, were never answered.

"We are satisfied that we have uncovered the 'truth' to the extent that it can be known," the commissioners concluded in their report.

But only one man knew the real truth of what happened to Leo LaChance inside the Northern Pawn and Gun Shop that cold winter night.

His name was Carney, but his friends called him Milt.

Hollywood Ending

IF IT HAD BEEN A MOVIE, THEY WOULD HAVE RUN INTO EACH other's arms, and shared a passionate embrace right in the middle of all those people.

But it wasn't like that at all.

Instead, Ken Rudolph stood in the baggage area of the Calgary International Airport alone, and scanned the crowd hopefully for the familiar face.

The Los Angeles filmmaker was looking forward to seeing his boyfriend. Laurence Jury had been gone for two months, having left the couple's home in Hollywood in mid-May to visit friends in Boston and Dallas, then heading out on a solo summer road trip through Canada. They had planned to meet in Calgary on July 11 and then go together to Vancouver for Expo '86.

But Jury wasn't at the airport.

It was possible he was running late, Rudolph knew. The two hadn't talked for about ten days, and Larry did like to have a good time. He could easily have gotten delayed or distracted somewhere along the line.

Rudolph collected his bags and took a cab to the hotel they had booked. He waited there alone for a couple of days, went on to Vancouver, then flew back to Los Angeles and filed a missing person report.

Rudolph was on the phone with Jury's sister when he got a call from a Los Angeles police officer bearing some gruesome news. Jury's body had been found along a highway in Canada. It was in Saskatchewan, near a place called Moose Jaw. The slender, handsome 37-year-old caterer and occasional interior designer had been stabbed at least twenty-two times, slashed twice on each cheek, five times on each side of his neck and on his chin, chest and shoulders. His right ear had been sliced from his head. Some of his stuff was found in the area a short time later— a yellow T-shirt with a picture of Pegasus on it, a pair of slim blue jeans, and a blood-soaked bag containing a gold T-shirt, a white and pink towel and musk cologne.

Jury's credit cards had been used to pay for a hotel room and buy some clothes at Woolco the day after his death, and someone continued to incur charges with them across the country—including two first-class plane tickets to the Maritimes.

The trail led police quickly to Roy Synette.

Synette was charged with first-degree murder, and police around the country started searching for the balding, heavy-set suspect. He was filling out welfare forms at Brandon City Hall when an RCMP officer approached and asked his name.

Synette was shaken and at first identified himself as Thomas Tunney, but the officer wasn't convinced. He demanded to see the man's tattoos. Synette rolled up his left sleeve and showed the officer two. One said "Born to Raise Hell," the other said "I'm Coming." When the officer demanded to see Synette's other arm, he slowly pulled up his sleeve and exposed a third tattoo. It said "Roy Synette."

"Roy Synette," the officer said. "You're under arrest for murder."

Still a drifter by middle age, Synette had been hitchhiking in Thunder Bay in early July when Jury offered him a ride. They drove west in Jury's little green hatchback, pulling into Regina on July 7 and then heading out together for a night on the town. They did the same the next night, pounding shooters at a downtown bar with two people they met on the street.

It was a wild couple of nights. Jury was boisterous and flamboyant, and having fun with his new friends.

"He wasn't ashamed at all," said Rick Lomas, a hairdresser who partied with Synette and Jury that night. "He was making it very obvious that he was a gay man."

Synette wasn't quite as lively. He was drinking heavily, becoming moody and dark.

On trial for Jury's murder, Synette said the two men were parked at the south edge of the city when Jury started caressing his leg. He said he slapped Jury and pushed him away, but when Jury started fingering his belt buckle, he lost it.

"From that point I just blew up and got really mad," he said. "It was like a bad movie."

Synette recalled stabbing Jury four or five times. Then he dumped Jury's body along the highway and drove toward Moose Jaw alone.

Defence lawyer Peter Kolenick argued the homosexual come-on provoked the killing, leaving the jury to decide whether a homosexual sexual advance was enough to make an ordinary person lose control and commit murder.

The jury decided it wasn't, and convicted Synette of second-degree murder.

Rudolph applauded the decision from the couple's home in California.

"The fact that it's not OK to kill a gay man just because he's gay is a good thing," he said.

The filmmaker agreed his boyfriend had been very sexual—so much so he had twice been entrapped by vice cops into committing lewd acts in public washrooms. Still, he said Jury had "totally cut back on that sort of thing" and would never have made unwanted sexual advances on a straight man.

"Life was his profession, it was his art," Rudolph said. "He was really brilliant at living. I'm sorry that his death was so violent and horrible."

A month after Roy Synette was convicted of murder in Jury's death, he pleaded guilty to manslaughter for stabbing a 39-year-old man at a house party a few weeks before he met Jury.

The Power of Persuasion

THE ONE-PAGE NOTE ADDRESSED TO THE UNIVERSITY OF NEW Orleans was printed on University of Regina letterhead. "I am submitting my updated curriculum vitae for your perusal and consideration for an academic position—tenure—in your facility," the cover letter began. "I am an assistant professor (since September 1998) in software systems engineering at the University of Regina (U of R). I have taught different undergraduate and graduate level courses, besides being an active researcher and administrator." In the final two paragraphs, the applicant further detailed her work and research. "I would welcome the opportunity of presenting one of my research works at your department and discussing my qualifications more fully with you," she concluded before signing "sincerely, Dr. Lana H. Nguyen."

Born and raised in Vietnam to parents who spent three years in a concentration camp, Nguyen had always worked hard to rise above her humble beginnings.

Her curriculum vitae reflected her dedication: a Bachelor of Science degree—*summa cum laude*—in electrical engineering in 1988, earned just three years after her family immigrated to Canada when she was 18; a doctorate in computer engineering in 1992; awards and scholarships;

and post-doctoral work in software systems engineering. Her resume showed she was also a member of several prestigious engineering societies.

And to the Dean of Engineering at the University of Regina, Nguyen's job application was proof the school's hard work was also paying dividends. "Nguyen's candidacy has been the fruit of our relentless proactive efforts in identifying potential women faculty members," Amit Chakma said in recommending her for the job.

It was a seller's market for engineering PhDs. This one came with glowing letters of reference from her previous employers, the University of Ottawa and Carleton University. The U of R had managed to attract a well-qualified applicant and a woman, at that, in a male-dominated field. In September 1998, Dr. Lana Nguyen became the new assistant professor of software engineering.

Inside her lab, Nguyen worked to create a computer chip that would compress Internet video files. Computer images that took half an hour to download, might take only ten minutes. And they would be better quality too, she promised.

Her project was called "Scalable Compression for Multi-Source Video Transmission." The university's new engineering professor had clearly impressed the National Sciences and Engineering Research Council of Canada. It awarded her a grant of $15,000 for each of four years to develop her chip.

But inside the classroom, her students were not nearly as impressed.

The pretty, petite professor with the shy smile was abrasive, belittling and sharp-tongued. Nguyen didn't spare her criticism of those who could not grasp what she called simple concepts. She berated her students as stupid and lazy. The professor argued with pupils over basic math. She blamed the university for failing to teach students the fundamentals.

But those students Nguyen called dumb could not help

but notice their professor copied notes straight from the textbook. The same could be said of the examples she used. And it took her an inordinate amount of time to return assignments. The students circulated petitions, pressing for her removal. One Monday morning, they just walked out of class *en masse*. Two other faculty members helped Nguyen teach the basic second-year course.

But it was not just the students who were complaining.

Nguyen's own colleagues found her difficult, aggressive, self-centred and temperamental. Some occasionally wondered about her apparent lack of knowledge of basic engineering principles, but chalked it up to her imperfect English.

When questions were raised about her abilities, the professor who was hired in an attempt to bring more women into the male-dominated faculty used her gender to her advantage. Nguyen hinted at harassment. The accusations kept her colleagues from digging deeper. She even put off a performance review because she didn't like the make-up of the committee. Nguyen did not think a mere lab instructor was qualified to judge her performance.

She did not need any review to tell her what she already knew for certain: she was working hard. She had taught more classes, and received positive student evaluations. She was bringing in research dollars. She was supervising aspiring PhDs. She even lobbied—albeit unsuccessfully—to get elected to the committee that reviewed job performance.

Two years into her career at the university, Nguyen wanted a promotion. She deserved it. That's when Dr. Ron Palmer, chair of the peer review committee, became suspicious of some of the claims in her application. He made a few phone calls. And Nguyen worked even harder.

The University of Ottawa had no record of her degree. Likewise, the University of Waterloo knew nothing of a Lana Nguyen receiving a doctorate. But there *was* a Hien Nguyen.

Lana H. Nguyen had an explanation. "Lana" was just the anglicized version of "Hien."

When that didn't work, Nguyen devised another plan. She tried to persuade Hien Nguyen's former supervising professor that she was one and the same person. Hien, she explained, had become Lana with a sex-change operation. But the real professor contacted the real Hien—the husband who had divorced Lana eight years earlier. Their marriage of less than a year ended shortly after Hien earned his engineering doctorate. Lana had been taking undergraduate science classes and did receive a bachelor degree.

Her ruse uncovered, Nguyen reacted with shock and outrage when the administration confronted her. She passionately denied having faked her credentials. Nguyen was given a week to establish the truth. Still proclaiming her innocence, she resigned in February 2001—before she could be fired.

Nguyen lost no time looking for work. She wrote her letter on March 4, 2001 to the University of New Orleans for an engineering position. She might have thought harder before using U of R letterhead. Checking references, the American university called her former employer. Nguyen did not get the job.

As it turned out, she probably would have had trouble getting across the border anyway. Two months after she resigned her U of R position, her fall from middle-class professor to pariah was complete. Dressed in a mint-green sweatsuit, the dainty Nguyen sat dejectedly in a courtroom prisoner's dock. She glared disdainfully at the media as once she had scorned her students.

The 34-year-old felon was unrepentant even after pleading guilty to impersonating her ex-husband and using his credentials to get hired by the U of R, receive federal research grants of about $30,000 and obtain engineering status. As a phoney professor, she had reaped nearly $166,000 in salary and benefits.

"I'm not ashamed of what I did. I'm proud of what I did," she boldly declared. Despite the lack of credentials, Nguyen believed she was qualified to do research and teach. She said she worked fourteen hours a day, seven days a week to prove her theories until "a piece of paper got in the way."

Justice Frank Gerein viewed the missing degree as more than mere paper. "You weaved a maze of lies and then persisted with them," said the judge who gave Nguyen a two-year sentence she could serve at home, instead of in a jail cell.

The search of Nguyen's residence that turned up hundreds of academic documents stolen from her ex-husband also uncovered a motivational book. It was written by the man who had authored *Advanced Formula for Total Success*, *How to Make the Impossible Possible*, and *50 Ideas That Can Change Your Life*.

There in Nguyen's house was the book that perhaps inspired her dedication, work ethic and hubris: *Dr. Robert Anthony's Magic Power of Super Persuasion*.

For Love for You

THE WEDDING WOULD TAKE PLACE IN SASKATOON LATE ON A Sunday, after the evening church service. It would be a small and simple affair, with only a handful of people there to witness the happy occasion, but it would be enough. They would be married, and that was all John Wilson wanted.

He met Jessie Patterson in 1916, shortly after he finished his training with the Royal North West Mounted Police and was dispatched to serve in Blaine Lake. It was the start of a bad time for the young officer. He contracted tuberculosis in 1917, and the Mounties discharged him when they found out about his illness—sending him away with only a tent and firm orders to quarantine himself.

If it hadn't been for Jessie and her family, John probably would have died that winter. The doctor certainly expected him to, and on many days John expected it himself. Though she was just a teenager, Jessie took care of him, applying poultices to his thin chest and back, nursing and caring for him when no one else would. She was always so good to him, better than anybody else. So kind and beautiful, he couldn't help but fall in love with her. She was his Jessie, and he wanted her to be his wife.

So, on a September day in 1918, John Wilson went to

Wheatley's Jewellery Store to get a marriage licence. He signed the licence with a flourish, and put the paper in his pocket for safekeeping.

The wedding day would arrive quickly.

Now all he had to do was get rid of his wife.

JOHN HAD WED MARY HUTCHISON—Polly, as most people called her—in Scotland ten years earlier, on the first day of 1908. She was cheerful and good-natured, a handsome woman with long sun-kissed curls, and John had courted her fiercely—even threatening to kill himself if he couldn't marry her.

The handsome young Scot won her over, and the intensity of his affections was contagious; Polly was soon so much in love she told a friend she would lay down her life if it would help him.

John headed off alone to Canada in the summer of 1912, hoping to find his fortune in Saskatoon. Promising he'd only be gone for a year, he left Polly with their young son, and six months pregnant with their second child.

At first John wrote a letter every Sunday and sent money home for his wife and children, but as time passed, his devotion began to fade. His letters home tapered off completely when he met Jessie in Blaine Lake. He was, it seemed, happy to leave the past behind him in Scotland.

Polly was not.

In the spring of 1918, nearly six years after her husband sailed away from her, Polly packed a suitcase and a trunk and boarded a luxury liner to Canada to find him. She arrived in Regina on April 18, after an overseas voyage and a cross-country train ride from Halifax, and soon tracked down her husband in the office of a Mountie superintendent in Prince Albert, where he was trying unsuccessfully to volunteer for an overseas cavalry unit.

John and Polly were reunited in Saskatoon the next day, and went back to Regina together to find a room to rent. Polly was pregnant again within days.

For months they survived that way, John working long hours at a new job with the military police, at times gone for days, while Polly waited for him alone at their Regina rooming house.

But still John couldn't forget his Jessie.

He continued to write to his pretty young girlfriend and travelled regularly to Blaine Lake to see her, all the while professing his love and swearing that rumours he was married were nonsense. By the time fall blew into the Prairies, he couldn't take it anymore.

On Monday, September 21, John was in Saskatoon dealing with a Doukhobor prisoner when he sat down and wrote two letters. One was to his wife, the other to Jessie.

In the first letter, John told his wife to take the train to Colonsay and said he would meet her at the station. She was five months pregnant by then, and he spoke about their future, and the life they would build together in Saskatoon.

"Polly, your old man is missing you and I know you are wearying also," he wrote. "I think you will like this place better than Regina, Polly, and I won't have to go out except very seldom."

The other letter was longer and even more affectionate. In it, he promised Jessie he was finalizing all the details for their wedding that weekend, and said he was going out that afternoon to pick up their marriage license.

"Sunday will soon be here when we shall be parted no more until death comes," he wrote.

He signed the letter "Your Loving, kind and true Jack boy."

Jack boy picked up Polly at the train station on the afternoon of September 27 as promised. She had dressed up for their reunion, and was wearing a fine blue wool suit and silk blouse with a fresh corsage pinned to her breast. They started off together in the car, heading first to Rosthern. John said he had business there.

As dusk crept in, John pulled over near Waldheim to

shoot two geese flying low along the train tracks. Then he turned to Polly, who was sitting on the front of the car looking at him, and shot her in the head with his double-barrelled shotgun.

John got a shovel and his gloves from the car, took a couple swigs of the booze he'd brought with him, and dug a hole four feet down in the soft earth. He took the $300 Polly had pinned to the corsage inside her shirt and both of her diamond wedding rings before pushing her body down into the fresh grave. He filled in the grave, then drove a short distance away and set the car on fire.

John was shoveling dirt on the vehicle when workers from a nearby threshing crew saw the flames and ran to the scene.

He told the men the car had caught fire while he was driving. As the farm workers helped put out the blaze, John was overcome. He staggered away from the fire and threw up along the side of the road, retching and gasping as the men looked on. His gun and suitcase sat in the grass beside the burning car.

When the fire was out, John hitched a ride into Blaine Lake with a family who lived in the area. Sitting in the backseat of the car with her brothers and sister, Agness Neufeldt noticed spatters of blood on the stranger's suitcase. When she asked him about it, he told her it was from the geese he had shot, and quickly pulled the bag into the front seat.

As John got out of the car, he gave the farmer a bit of money and the shovel.

"I have no further use for it," he said.

Then he went to Jessie.

They were married two days later, in a small ceremony at Knox Presbyterian Church in Saskatoon. Jessie's parents and her brother were there, and it was all John could have hoped. From that day on he would do everything he could for his wee girlie.

John joined the Mounties again, and after surviving the

flu pandemic together the couple moved to Vancouver, where John was assigned to undercover work. They were wonderfully happy, but Jessie knew there was something wrong. Her husband would at times become quiet and withdrawn, his face clouded with some dark thought. No matter how many times she asked, he would never tell her what he was thinking about.

She would find out soon enough.

Far away in Carluke, Scotland, Polly's family also sensed there was something wrong. Polly hadn't written for months, and the telegrams and letters they received from John were confusing and upsetting. In one, he said Polly had nearly died in the pandemic and he was terminally ill. In another, he said they were sailing immediately home to Scotland.

He'd told other people Polly was severely injured in a car accident.

Searching for the truth, Polly's sister, Elizabeth Craig, began sending frantic letters to everyone who may have come in contact with the couple.

"Could you get the information from another source than Wilson as we would have no faith now in anything he told us about my sister—he always was a plausible liar," Elizabeth wrote in a letter to Mounted Police Superintendant Walton Routledge.

But a police officer who looked into the matter for Routledge concluded everything was fine. John Wilson's wife was perfectly well and living with her husband in Vancouver; the officer had seen her himself.

Then Elizabeth sent a picture of her missing sister. It wasn't the same woman.

After a quiet investigation, Sergeant John Wilson was ordered to return to Saskatchewan for a new assignment. He was taken into custody at the Regina train station on November 10, 1919, and immediately stripped of his status as an officer.

Then he was charged with murder.

John denied it at first and tried to kill himself in his jail cell, slashing his throat from ear to ear with a pocketknife. He lived and later confessed to the crime, even telling police where to find Polly's shallow grave. Her body was found at that spot on December 12, decomposed, her skull shattered. The coroner who performed an autopsy noted her good, healthy heart.

Though he claimed Polly's death was an accident, John Wilson was convicted of murder and sentenced to hang. He died on April 23, 1920, the same day Jessie gave birth to his son.

Before he died, he apologized to the woman he loved—but not to the one he had killed.

"God knows I done this lassie wrong but every minute of the fourteen months I was with her were happiness to me in spite of my worry," he wrote, in one of his three statements to police. "She is far and above any girl I ever met, honest, true and kind, and she never knew what I had to do to gain her. I had it in my mind that I must marry her legally and I done it.

"Jessie this is near the end, and when you read this, it was my love for you, all this. And dearest wifie, although I have ruined your life, it was done for love for you."

In His Mind

DRUGS ON THE DOORKNOBS. Cars trying to gas him. Poison in his shaving cream.

And when none of those things worked, they went after his food.

Someone was trying to kill Ziadten Abdelmajid Boughanmi.

And while the bright foreign exchange student didn't know precisely who, he knew the what and the why. Ziadten could communicate directly with God. And that made him a target. An Israeli extremist group was plotting to assassinate him. But the who—that was a little more difficult to answer. Any number of people might be part of the conspiracy: security guards, professors, doctors or even store clerks.

Ziadten couldn't be too careful.

He barricaded himself in lecture rooms at the University of Ottawa and tussled with campus security who accused him of trespassing at night. Ziadten, the son of two doctors back in Tunisia, had come to the university in 1985 on a scholarship. The electrical engineering student knew at least three languages and excelled on the computers. Few people noticed, however, because Ziadten was so quiet and shy. He became even more of an introvert after his mother was killed in a traffic accident a year into his studies in Canada.

Four years after coming to Ottawa, Ziadten knew he had to leave. The people who wanted him dead were closing in.

He applied for entrance to the University of Regina in January 1989 and took a small, third-floor apartment suite the next month. A few weeks later when his landlady opened the door, she was assaulted by an overwhelming stench. It emanated from the refrigerator that did not refrigerate. The power had never been turned on.

Cans of food, pried open with a knife, had barely been tasted, then left to rot. Ziadten knew the food had been poisoned too. The 23-year-old student had run away—but they had found him. The knife marks in the walls and the broken window were evidence of his struggle to defend himself.

His landlady grudgingly cleaned. Stiffed by another deadbeat tenant, she thought. But Ziadten came back and was infuriated by her touching his possessions. He dumped the bags of garbage on the floor. Looking for what, she could never be sure. There were no clothes, no dishes, nothing personal in the apartment.

The one thing Ziadten did own was a large, heavy grey parka. He kept it zipped to the neck with the hood pulled up over his wavy black hair. It was the coat that immediately caught the loss-prevention officer's attention when Ziadten walked into the department store. It was Tuesday, April 25, 1989, with temperatures hovering in the mid-teens. Whenever anyone came near Ziadten, he would hunch his shoulders, pulling his head deeper into the coat. He looked like a classic shoplifter—dodgy and skittish. Roaming through men's wear, Ziadten picked up a shirt and tentatively approached the cashiers. But he couldn't settle on exactly the right check-out. He put the shirt back. The officer had seen enough. He asked Ziadten to leave the store.

Ziadten didn't go far. He joined the line-up across the street at the bank and waited his turn. But as he got closer to the tellers, things didn't feel right. He walked out the door, only to get back in line again moments later. Bank staff called police.

The officers thought it odd that Ziadten was wearing his parka—but odd is not against the law. Nor was the knife he carried in his pocket. It was a souvenir from his time in Ottawa. In his broken English, Ziadten apologized for his actions. It was not his usual bank. He was simply confused.

He was allowed to walk away.

The next day, Ziadten went to Safeway to buy cooking oil. When the cashier grasped the bottle, he grabbed it back and got another one from the shelf. But his diligence had made no difference.

Back at his apartment, his eyes became twisted and he grew tired after using the oil. He though the poison might be a drug, like a steroid. Ziadten sensed the presence of God. "You have to kill her," God directed. He had to defend himself from the people poisoning his food.

Ziadten put on his parka and returned to the same grocery store two days later. He stood by the payphone for nearly half an hour, picking up the receiver, plugging in his coins, but talking to no one.

Shirley Mae Grant arrived to relieve her co-worker in the express lane sometime around noon on that fateful Friday. Shirley was 47 years old, married, and the mother of a daughter and son. She was pleasant and easy-going; most of her customers appreciated her friendly banter.

Ziadten got into her line and placed his grocery items on the counter. As she had done hundreds of times in her sixteen-year career, Shirley dragged the purchases across the bar code scanner. She then handed Ziadten his change.

"Have a nice day," she said. Shirley was friendly. Courteous. Innocent.

But in Ziadten's mind, she was none of those things. As

he saw it, Shirley was mocking him. And she was poisoning his food.

Ziadten looked at the cashier, and saw her face grow distorted. Shirley was the devil. And the voice of God—for Ziadten had no doubt that was who uttered the words only he could hear—commanded him to kill her.

The slight, shy student looked so calm. Except for his dark eyes. They were wild.

Ziadten pulled his souvenir knife from his right pocket. He plunged the blade into Shirley's upper chest. The poor woman was dead before she arrived at the hospital. The knife had hit a main artery.

Secure in the fact he had done as God had asked, Ziadten calmly strode out of the store. Police caught up to him a few blocks away. Ziadten stared vacantly at the officers.

"I saw her as a strange creator [sic], as a devil," he said. "As if God ordered me to kill her. Creator [sic] no good."

Even in the psychiatric unit that temporarily became his home, Ziadten couldn't be too careful. He stopped eating again. But Ziadten was a smart man. His religion forbade him to eat pork, so no one would think to poison that meat. Having outwitted his adversaries, Ziadten ate pork.

They were all in on it—from the lawyer who said he represented his interests, to the doctors who claimed they wanted to help him. They even lied about the cashier—showing him a newspaper story about her death. She wasn't dead. He knew it. At most, he could be charged with armed assault; but he had acted in self defence.

Ziadten refused to take their pills. So the doctors gave him injections. In time, blunted by the anti-psychotic drugs, the voices were more difficult to hear. But they were never far away. Even the doctors knew that.

"If he didn't get the medication, I'm sure he would revert to the hallucinatory, delusional state he was in," said one psychologist. With his demons medicated, Ziadten could be friendly and personable. Maybe benign.

And eighteen months after Shirley was murdered in what should have been the safest of jobs, her killer was deemed fit to stand trial.

The hearing was only a formality. The prosecutor, the defence lawyer, the psychiatrists and the judge knew Ziadten was not guilty by reason of insanity. "I can only describe him as a very tortured person," Justice Joseph McIntyre said. "The sad part of the whole thing is that anybody whom he associated with when he met them more than once or twice immediately became, in his mind, part of the conspiracy to poison him or to take his life." Ziadten remained in Saskatchewan in a secure psychiatric centre until immigration authorities deported him on Halloween day 1991.

Some people Ziadten had met in church recognized long before the court's pronouncement that he was more than confused or odd. Ziadten was ill. They had tried to help, believing it best if he returned home to his family. They bought him a plane ticket back to Tunisia.

Ziadten had been set to fly back to his North African homeland on April 29, 1989. The day before he was to leave, the man who believed he was God's messenger killed the woman he thought was the devil in Safeway.

It Would Explode the Heart

EVERYONE WAS SLEEPING.

Randy Kaminskas lay sprawled on the bed, alone in the space he normally shared with his wife, Gladys, who was at work that night. Ten-year-old Aaron was sound asleep in his bedroom, and the twins, Ali and Andrea, were curled up in their bunk beds with the remnants of a late-night snack — potato chips and an orange — littering their room.

The family dog, Tex, snoozed on the floor.

It was June 15, 1997. Father's Day, a day the Kaminskas family had planned to spend planting trees together in the yard of their Martensville bungalow. Instead, the day began with a scream.

Scrambling out of bed and racing into his daughters' darkened bedroom, Randy found a man standing beside the girls' bunk beds. He recognized the man as a friend of his older daughter, Alica, who was out of town at a wedding.

"You're James, aren't you?" Randy demanded of the intruder.

When the man said yes, Randy led him angrily out of the house, pushing him out the door and into the night.

Randy rushed back to the girls' bedroom to make sure they were okay. He found Ali cowering under her blanket on the top bunk, while Andrea lay still and silent on the bottom bed.

Reaching for Andrea Randy felt the wetness of her pyjamas and, turning on the light, was horrified to discover they were drenched with blood. He raced to the phone to call 9-1-1 and tried to save her life, but it was no use. His little girl had been stabbed once through the heart, the knife penetrating her small body all the way to her spine.

WITHIN HOURS, POLICE ARRESTED 18-year-old James Woloschuk, a former high school football star, and charged him with first-degree murder. The arrest was an immediate relief not only to the Kaminskas family, but to the entire community of Martensville, left reeling by the shocking and violent death of a happy Grade 2 student, brutally murdered in her own bed. The relief was short-lived.

The charge against Woloschuk was dropped the next day, when a computer and security camera in the lobby of the Saskatoon hotel where the teen worked proved he was on shift when Andrea was murdered.

With Woloschuk cleared, Randy Kaminskas became the prime suspect in his daughter's death.

While police searched for evidence, locals convicted the construction worker over coffee and neighbours fell silent when Kaminskas came near. Relatives of Randy's who went to RCMP headquarters to convince investigators of his innocence left the building believing otherwise. After discussing the case with police, even Gladys Kaminskas was sure of her husband's guilt.

Now all the police had to do was prove it.

Then, three weeks later, Tara Kroeker was stabbed.

The 19-year-old lived and worked in Saskatoon, but was home for a weekend visit. Leaving the Martensville Sports Bar around closing time on July 5, she was joined by one of her brother's friends, Nathan Oxby.

Despite being known around town as a loner and sometime bully, Oxby was in good spirits that night, smiling and laughing as he left the bar and joined up with Kroeker for the walk home.

As they strolled together down the darkened streets, Oxby lagged behind for a moment. Kroeker felt a searing pain as he plunged a knife deep into her back. When she screamed and started to run, Oxby grabbed her and tried to stab her again.

"Please help me," she yelled, as the two tussled in an alley. "He's trying to kill me."

Oxby covered Kroeker's mouth with his hand and she bit down hard on one of his fingers, holding on tightly with her teeth while she tried to wrestle the knife away from him. Oxby didn't give it up easily, punching and slashing at her again and again, cutting and scraping her hand, arm, face and eye.

When the pain in his finger became too intense to bear, Oxby begged Kroeker to let go, promising he'd leave her alone. When she loosened her bite, he kicked her in the face and ran away. Kroeker ran too, racing to her brother's house for help.

Five minutes later, when two nearby residents finally emerged from their houses to see what was happening, the alley was empty.

Kroeker told police Oxby had attacked her, and gave investigators the knife he'd stabbed her with. It was the same kind of serrated, wood-handled steak knife that had been used to kill Andrea Kaminskas, and matched a set that had been stolen from a drawer in the Kaminskas' kitchen after Andrea's murder.

Oxby's fingerprints were on the drawer.

Police in the area already knew Oxby. They'd been having trouble with him for years, and he'd recently been charged with sexually assaulting a 2-year-old girl in nearby Warman.

Interrogated by RCMP Corporal Ken Homeniuk in

Saskatoon, the clean-cut 19-year-old farmhand at first denied having anything to do with Kaminskas' death. Then he said he did it, but maintained it was an accident.

Oxby said Alica Kaminskas had asked him to check on her younger sisters while she was away, and he was doing that when he tripped on a toy and found a knife on the floor. He picked the knife up and then he stumbled, he said. He hit his head and landed right on top of the little girl.

"I had this stupid knife in my hand and I was gonna stick it in the kitchen I guess, but I never made it there ...," he told Homeniuk. "I remember I stuck both hands out, an' I had the knife in this hand, and then I just—she was there. Just right there."

Oxby said he even tried to help the injured girl, and plugged the hole in her chest for a while with his finger to slow the bleeding, but then Randy came and dragged him out of the house.

"I can't kill anybody," Oxby said. "If a guy's pissin' me off I'll punch the ever-lovin' shit outta him, but once he's down I just, I quit, and then I feel bad the next day."

He said even shooting a rabbit or gopher was hard for him.

"I get this nervous scared gut feeling in me," he said. "And I hesitate before I actually pull the trigger."

Oxby suggested Alica's old boyfriend, who had a similar haircut and was the same height as him, may have committed the murder.

The person who did it could be a psycho or a pencil pusher, he said. Either way, he believed the killer should get lethal injection for killing an innocent 8-year-old girl.

"He's probably a nervous wreck and he's wondering when he's going to get caught," Oxby speculated. "Or probably just sitting there, 'Yeah, I haven't got caught. I can try this again.'"

"So you figure this guy would try this again if he got away with it once?" Homeniuk asked.

Oxby said yes.

"Well if you stole from a store and you never got caught you'd try it again, wouldn't you?"

In fact, that's exactly what Oxby had done after the little girl's murder—though his memories of Kroeker's stabbing were dim.

"All's I know is next thing you know she was on the ground...," he told Homeniuk. "I guess I stabbed her then, I don't know."

Oxby couldn't even remember what kind of knife he used.

"Beats the ever-livin' piss outta me," he said.

LONG BEFORE HE WAS A dangerous man, Nathan Oxby was a troubled boy.

A hyperactive child from a broken home, Oxby's violent tendencies and quick temper were cause for alarm from an early age. By the time he turned 8, school authorities were concerned enough to send Oxby to a child psychologist, who reported that the boy was prone to strange and violent fantasies—many of which were graphically sexual or involved super-human feats far beyond the fantasies of other boys his age.

"Nathan becomes so caught up in these descriptions of impossible events that it is my feeling that he slips into this world much too comfortably and completely," psychologist Ken Ahlers wrote in the fall of 1986.

Five years later, as Oxby entered his teen years, the problems were getting worse. He'd started drinking and strangling himself to get high, and continued to live in fantasy worlds where he was superior to those around him. He didn't get along well with other kids or authority figures and had trouble with the law, stealing money and cigarettes, joy riding, racking up charges for assault, robbery and mischief.

Reports by psychologists and psychiatrists prepared in those days painted a grim picture of a growing problem: A boy boastful about his ability to inflict pain, quick to lie and manipulate, with no regard for the rights or feelings of others. A boy that could do terrible things.

And he did.

Early in 1999, Oxby appeared in a Saskatoon courtroom and pleaded guilty to second-degree murder in Andrea Kaminskas' death and aggravated assault for stabbing Kroeker. He was sentenced to life in prison with no chance of parole for twenty years.

"Nathan wasn't born evil," his lawyer Darren Hagen said. "Babies aren't evil. Somewhere along the line something has gone drastically wrong with this young lad."

During his sentencing Oxby was cool and calm, showing nothing. He had tried to commit suicide while in custody, and told the Kaminskas family about it in court as proof of his remorse.

"I took the sum of almost 200 pills," he said. "It would speed the heart and it would explode the heart. I did that on behalf of Andrea, I just can't live with this. It's just as bad as you guys."

It wasn't.

Seventeen months after Andrea's death, Randy remained haunted by the vision of his daughter stabbed through the heart, her life ebbing away before him. Ali, at the age of 9, was scared to sleep by herself, anguished at the death of her twin sister and best friend. Worst of all, the family could find no reason for the young girl's murder.

"Why did you take her life?" Andrea's older brother, Aaron, asked Oxby in court. "Did you even have a reason?"

He never got an answer.

The Darkness of the Night

THE DARKNESS CAME SLOWLY AND PAINFULLY, BURNING ITS way in from the corners until it consumed everything. Most days the pain was so intense it felt like it was driving him crazy. He couldn't read anymore, it hurt too much. Sometimes he couldn't even sleep, and instead spent the nights smoking cigarettes and pacing around his small room, trying to forget about the horrible burning in his eyes, and the blackness that was coming with it.

ALEXANDER OSHUK WAS A NICE MAN, good-tempered, likeable and well-read. In his early 30s, the Ukrainian immigrant was a leader in Moose Jaw's communist movement, respected by his countrymen and others in the community. He made a good living waiting tables at the Paris Café, the Savoy, and the Princess Restaurant, and took theatrical roles with the Ukrainian Dramatic Society.

"I could say he was the best man on earth," said John Kozen, a longtime friend who once roomed with Oshuk.

Others said the same about Dr. William Brown.

After setting up practice in Moose Jaw in 1900, Brown became one of the most highly respected doctors in the area, and was popular among his peers and patients. Brown further distinguished himself serving overseas in the Great War, where his bravery at the Battle of the

Somme in 1916 earned him the prestigious Military Cross. He was also a longtime Freemason.

As he approached his 61st birthday, Brown remained a practising doctor and a strong, able-bodied man, capable of withstanding even the rigours of the Moose Jaw golf course, a hilly and strenuous course too demanding for a man of delicate health.

Oshuk went to see Dr. Brown for the first time early in 1925, after finding himself in the unfortunate position of having been infected with a sexually transmitted disease. At first Oshuk wasn't overly concerned; he'd had gonorrhoea a few years earlier, and it had been cleared up quickly enough. Dr. Brown immediately started Oshuk on an intensive course of treatment. Months later, the infection lingered and Oshuk's eyes had begun to bother him.

When Oshuk told the doctor about his eye problems, Brown prescribed a black, foul smelling eyewash he promised would clear up the problem. The lotion burned and stung, but Oshuk continued the treatment, desperate to clear up the condition. He'd been courting a girl in Winnipeg, but knew he couldn't marry her until he was cured.

But two years later, his infection persisted, and his eyes were worse than ever.

He was haunted by the idea of going blind; he knew what kind of life a blind man faced. He worried about being shunned by society, and was afraid of being helpless and an outcast. Already unable to work much of the time, Oshuk had been borrowing money from friends to survive. If his eyes could not be fixed, his future would depend entirely on the charity of others.

Doctors in Regina and Swift Current examined Oshuk's eyes but offered little hope. His last chance, a specialist in Rochester, gave him an equally grim prognosis.

Oshuk ran into his friend Kozen on the street after returning to Moose Jaw.

"Told me the same thing as the rest of the doctors,"

Oshuk said. "My eyes was ruined and burned by the medicine. The glands was burned."

Oshuk said the doctors told him his eyes were eventually going to burst and would leak out through the burned glands, causing total blindness.

He tried to get prominent Moose Jaw lawyer Oswold Regan to represent him in a $5,000-lawsuit against the doctor. At first it seemed Regan would take the case, but after considering the matter for several months he turned it down, saying he could not take action against a professional. Plus, Regan had known the doctor since before the war, and knew him to be a good man. The two still played golf together.

The Law Society in turn refused to move against Regan, and by then it had taken too long to do anything at all.

"They squashed everything," Oshuk told Kozen.

The hopelessness of his situation was weighing heavily on Oshuk when he saw his friend John Wasley in the summer of 1927.

"There is no justice in this world at all," Oshuk said.

A few weeks later, he started carrying the gun. He wasn't sure what he was going to do with it at first, he just tucked it into the waistband of his pants and kept it with him for a while.

Then, on the afternoon of October 3, after having lunch at the Maple Leaf Café, Oshuk walked down Main Street and into the Hammond Building. It was shortly after 4:00 p.m. when he climbed the stairs leading toward Dr. Brown's office.

Oshuk found the doctor sitting at his desk, reading a magazine and smoking his pipe. He left him nearly the same way a moment later—but for a single bullet hole in the left breast of the doctor's blue suit and the spattering of ash that had sprinkled out of his pipe when it fell to the floor.

The sound of the gunshot reverberated through the second floor, sounding to some in the building like an explosion, to others like a board falling flat in the hallway. By the time Brown's colleagues and friends ran into the room, he was dead.

Oshuk walked calmly but quickly out of the building and down Main Street.

Oswold Regan was leaving his law office in the Woolworth building when he stopped to talk to his wife, Margaret, about a dictation she had taken incorrectly. He was standing behind her watching her type when Oshuk walked in with the gun.

Lifting the weapon and pointing it squarely at Oswold, Oshuk spoke.

"I've shot Dr. Brown," he said. "And I have come to shoot you."

While the lawyer scrambled to hide under his wife's desk, Margaret stood up and confronted the intruder.

"You can't shoot him," she said firmly. "You'll have to shoot me first."

For an instant everything stopped.

Oshuk looked at the woman, and she returned his gaze, unblinking. Then he lowered the gun. He was suddenly very meek and calm.

"No, I can't shoot you, Mrs. Regan," he said.

With that, Oshuk broke open the weapon, took out the spent cartridge which had been used against Dr. Brown, and dumped out five more unfired rounds onto Margaret Regan's desk.

"You're saved," he told Oswold. "This woman has saved you."

Oshuk sat down and talked quietly with Margaret until the police arrived to arrest him. He talked to her about the problems with his eyes.

"He wasn't the same man that I had known before," she said later, recalling their conversation. "Didn't seem to be at all."

Oshuk was tried by jury in January 1928, before a crowd that packed the Moose Jaw courtroom and spilled out into the hallways and corridors. Some men crouched on the windowsills of the courthouse to see the proceedings.

Oshuk sat expressionless throughout the trial, always clean-shaven with his hair brushed back from his face in a neat pompadour, while his lawyer, Walter Mills, made an impassioned case for mercy.

Mills argued Oshuk wasn't sane when he committed the murders, and had been driven temporarily mad by his ill health, bitterness and impending blindness.

"Think of him as he was, his eyes affected in consequence of the lotion that the doctor had used on him. No day time for him, but always the darkness of the night …," Mills told the hushed crowd during his closing argument. "It maddened him and he becomes a madman bereft of control, unable to choose between right and wrong."

The jury didn't see it that way.

Oshuk was convicted of murder and sentenced to die. He didn't flinch when the fatal sentence was delivered, and as he was led out of the courtroom he turned and waved his hat to some friends.

At 5:00 a.m. on April 26, Oshuk walked up the scaffold at Regina jail alone.

"I have no fear," he said.

The trap was sprung.

And then, darkness.

Black and Blue

IT WAS LATE WHEN THE PHONE RANG IN JIM EDWARDS' Saskatoon apartment. A young man was on the line, and Edwards hung up. The phone rang again and again after that, but Edwards let his answering machine pick it up each time. Finally, the caller left a message. It was a rock song called Hey Piggy, blaring loud and distorted through the phone.

"Black and blue and broken bones, you've left me here I'm all alone," the singer wailed. "Nothing can stop me now because I don't care anymore."

Edwards knew the message was from her.

He had met Adele Andre in 1994 at St. Mark's, an inner-city Saskatoon school where he taught fourth grade. She came in one day with her two daughters saying she planned to register them at the school, and Edwards showed the three of them around.

Edwards and Andre spent about five minutes together.

Soon after that, the cards started coming. There were gifts too, and phone calls to the school. Edwards returned the presents, threw out the cards and tried to avoid contact with the woman, enlisting the help of other teachers to keep them apart when she came around.

One day Andre left him a tin box full of gumballs and a note.

"I miss seeing you very much," the note read. "Much love, Adele."

Edwards was driving home from school one night when Andre pulled up beside him on the road.

" I won't bother you anymore," she promised, yelling to him from her car. He drove away.

Then the phone calls had started. Usually they were hang-ups, but sometimes he could hear giggling or laughing on the other end. Sometimes there were threats, too, warnings to watch his back. The people threatening him sounded like children.

THOUGH HE DIDN'T KNOW IT, Edwards' life became very dangerous one November night in 1997, as a group of teenage girls sat around Adele Andre's house watching TV, hanging out and talking.

It was a normal night. Both of the 14-year-old guests, Christa and Becky, were good friends of Andre's teenage daughter, and they liked spending time with Andre. She was cool for a mom. She let them hang out at her house, even told them it was okay if they wanted to smoke pot there.

Sometime that November evening, Andre told the girls she'd like to slash a guy's tires. Becky and Christa quickly volunteered to do the job, but Andre told them she wanted some older boys to do it instead. She'd even pay.

When Becky said she knew a few guys who would probably slash tires for a bit of money, Andre asked whether they would break someone's kneecaps, too.

Becky thought they would, and she was right.

Two days later, Becky's brother Dustin, his friends Brad and Ryan, and an older guy named Ashley went to Andre's house after school and listened to what she had to say. Andre told the teens she wanted to hurt a guy who had molested her daughters and gotten them taken away from her. The guy had kidnapped her daughter and put her through a series of experimental drugs and probes, she said.

She wanted his truck smashed, his wife beaten up and his house vandalized. Then she said she wanted him killed.

"I thought it was stupid," Becky said later. "Like, I don't mind that they wanted to beat him up, but I just thought that killing him is a little harsh."

Harsh or not, some of the teens, including Becky's brother, were willing to consider it.

"I was thinking about it," Dustin admitted. "But I never actually said yes... She had me believing about the stories."

Ashley Weber considered it too. He got angry when he heard that this guy had raped Andre's daughter, and thought the guy deserved to be punished. Also, it would be easy money. Andre had, at various times, offered the teens anywhere from $200 to $3,000 for the job, depending on what they were willing to do to Edwards. If they were willing to kill him she'd pay the most, and said she'd provide the gun and some special bullets she promised were untraceable by police.

The money convinced Ryan.

He agreed to beat Edwards up for a few hundred bucks, and later agreed to kill him because "$3,000 started to sound pretty good."

Everything was ready to go ahead, but Ryan started to have second thoughts about the plan—and about Andre.

"She started acting a little strange. I don't know how I'd explain it," he said. "Just small things. She started talking about this Jim guy and the things he'd done and it started to sound a little strange."

The rest of the teens turned on Andre when she accused them of stealing clothes, food and feminine hygiene products from her house.

"She called us and said, 'Yeah, my pants are missing,'" Becky said. "She said they were black leather pants or something, that cost like $3,000. She said that we used up all her $300 perfume, and that we took her pads and her tampons and her pantyliners and like 500 pounds of meat."

After the teens pulled out of the plot, Andre pitched it to another aquaintance, offering David Dumais $1,000 to break Edwards' kneecaps with a bat. She told Dumais that Edwards had molested her daughters and forced her to have an abortion, and had been stalking her for years.

But even as Andre conspired to hurt Edwards, still she volleyed between love and hate. She told Dumais she had a deep psychic connection with Edwards and was marrying him. She even modelled a wedding dress and veil for Dumais, twirling around the livingroom in her long white dress and a pair of red socks.

"She talked about wanting to be with him as a couple," Dumais said. "She liked him. She said she found him attractive. He was athletic and all that, I guess, and this basically is how she described him all the time. But at the same time she was angry at him because he wasn't paying any attention to her."

The only time Edwards and Andre were together was when they met in a courtroom.

There Andre was convicted of counseling three youths and an adult to commit murder and assault, and mischief. She was also found guilty of extortion for blackmailing a married business man she had sex with outside a convenience store in an attempt to get money to pay her legal bills. She was sentenced to two years in prison.

"I don't know which I find more appalling," said Justice Ted Malone, "the accused's request, or the fact one of the teenagers considered beating up the victim, but she thought killing him was 'a little harsh.'"

Jim Edwards is a pseudonym, as are Becky, Christa, Dustin and Brad. A court order prohibits publication of any information which would identify the victim or youths.

No Place for Serenity

THE TWO TEENS SPLASHED AROUND IN THE HOTEL SWIMMING pool with the little girl, all three bobbing up and down in the turquoise-tinted water. They'd been in there for hours, their fingers wrinkled, the smell of chlorine all around them.

The man had been watching them for a while, staring intently as the girls paddled in the middle of the open water. The older ones looked like they were 12 or 13, girls just turning into women, and the one they were with was just a little kid. Barely more than a baby.

Something about it wasn't right.

At first the man couldn't be sure, but he thought the teens were dunking the toddler in the water on purpose, sometimes leaving her in the middle of the deep end and making her paddle back to the pool's edge. Whenever the child got to the edge of the pool, the older girls pulled her back out to the middle again. The toddler looked tired and scared, and was spitting up water.

Finally the man approached and told the girls to stop.

"She has to learn to swim," one of them snapped at him.

On the second day the teens amused themselves with the game, 3-year-old Scentri Fox drowned. Her babysitters were charged with criminal negligence and manslaughter.

SERENA LEE NICOTINE WAS a beautiful girl, with full lips, high, round cheeks and wide brown eyes that never showed the trouble inside. Trouble which began long before she was born.

Her mother Melvina had a tough life and drank heavily, even as Serena kicked and grew inside Melvina's swelling belly in the long cool fall of 1981. Serena paid the price for her mother's problems. She came screaming into the world on January 23, 1982, her brain severely damaged by fetal alcohol syndrome.

Her life got worse from there.

Raised in North Battleford by her mother and some uncles, Serena Nicotine learned early how to drink and do drugs, but received little guidance in other areas.

As a child she watched a man get murdered, saw her mother stab her grandfather in the chest with a butcher knife, and stood by helplessly as her stepfather got choked unconscious.

When there were people in the house partying—as there so often were—Nicotine would go around collecting knives and hiding them under the bed so no one would get hurt. She quit school in Grade 6, and spent her days playing bingo with her mom, going to Wal-Mart and stealing wallets to get drinking money.

By the time she was 12 and old enough to be charged, Nicotine had already had many run-ins with the law, including falsely reporting herself to have been kidnapped, and had become one of the best-known youths in the community. She became even better known a year later, when she took Scentri Fox for a deadly swim in the pool at the Happy Inn Hotel.

"We better stop lying to the police," Nicotine wrote in a letter to her 12-year-old co-accused while in jail awaiting their trial.

"I really remember what happened. I could picture us holding her down in the water counting up to forty or fifty and all. But we didn't beat her up or anything, all we did was drown her."

The letter sealed Nicotine's conviction, and she was sentenced to two years in jail. Her friend was found not guilty.

Nicotine's lawyer, Scott Hopley, said the tragedy of the case began with his client's horrible life.

"Every person or agency who had some sort of responsibility to this young girl has dropped the ball," he said.

A psychologist who conducted tests on Nicotine remarked on the teen's deeply disturbed view of the world.

"Serena's stories were the most violent that I have ever heard in response to this test," said psychologist Josephine Nanson. "Every story was marked by extreme violence or other adverse events. Nicotine sees the world as an ugly, fearful place, where the overriding theme is violence."

Nicotine spent the first fifteen months of her manslaughter sentence at a youth centre in Regina before moving to a halfway house in North Battleford, a private home operated by 58-year-old Helen Montgomery.

Nicotine arrived at Montgomery's house on December 17, 1997, and was introduced to another girl, Cathy Gail Mackenzie, who was serving a four-month sentence for robbing a gas station.

If anyone could help the troubled young girls, Montgomery could. She had taken the pain of her own polio-ravaged life and turned it into a passion for helping young people, and had welcomed countless troubled kids into her modest North Battleford bungalow. Montgomery's friends described her as a caring woman who always looked for the best in people.

The same could not be said for Mackenzie and Nicotine.

Mackenzie had been living at the house for less than a month and had already been fighting with Montgomery about smoking inside the house. The teen was fed up with the place—and with Montgomery.

Mackenzie and Nicotine hit it off right away. A day

after Nicotine arrived, the two 15-year-olds were sitting at the dining room table like best friends, passing notes back and forth while Montgomery relaxed nearby in her favourite armchair.

In one note Mackenzie called Montgomery a "fat-ass no good for nothing," and in another referred to her as "a white piece of trash."

Then Mackenzie told Nicotine to start a fight with the woman.

"Call her a bitch and I'll go get the frying pan," she wrote, passing the note along the table to Nicotine.

Within moments the girls were writing another note, leaving it beside Montgomery's battered body for the police to find.

"Hey Pigs," it said. "Well fuck you all 'cause what's done is done. We can't undo this shit. She's a fat worthless bitch. If she's dead, we didn't mean to kill her, we just wanted to knock the bitch out. She shouldn't fuck with us. She doesn't know who she's messing with. So probably by the time you get this letter, we'll be long gone. We just need some fucking freedom. We're getting deadly cravings for drugs. If we had drugs, we'd be alright. Did you ever have a withdrawal? Probably not but we need some drugs. BAD. You should have put me in narcotics abuse sooner. It's all your guy's fault. You made us do it you fuckin' pigs."

Then the teens took Montgomery's money and revved up her car, driving it through the garage door and fleeing to Saskatoon and then to Prince Albert.

Montgomery died in her armchair. She had been stabbed and slashed fifteen times with one of the knives from her kitchen and bludgeoned with her cast iron frying pan.

Her daughter found the body the next day.

"It made me feel like there was an erupting volcano inside me," said Valerie Montgomery-Bull, recalling the bloody scene. "When I picked up the phone to dial 9-1-1, I got some of my mother's blood on my hands."

The teen killers were arrested at a mall in Prince Albert. Sixteen days before her 16th birthday, Nicotine was charged with murder.

She pleaded guilty to second-degree murder that spring, and was sentenced to life in prison with no chance of parole for seven years. Because of her age, it was the maximum sentence that could have been imposed. Nicotine would start her sentence at the Regional Psychiatric Centre in Saskatoon, the only facility in the province equipped to deal with the young killer.

During sentencing, Justice Gene Ann Smith said Nicotine had not received any of the nurturing or teaching children require, and functioned at the level of a six-year-old.

"The indisputable fact is Ms. Nicotine represents a very considerable danger to the public and herself," Smith said.

The words were a grim prediction of what was to come.

A year later, Nicotine and another teenage prisoner, 19-year-old Meagan Jan Hicks, went into the nurse's station at the Psychiatric Centre armed with a large serrated knife and demanded to make phone calls to their boyfriends in other correctional facilities.

They grabbed a nurse, tied the woman up with an extension cord, and blindfolded her.

"You'd better phone your family because it's the last time you're going to see them," Nicotine advised. "You're leaving here in a black bag."

They all knew it was not an empty threat.

"I'm a killer," Nicotine told the nurse. "You people all think I'm a nice little girl. What do I have to lose?"

They held the nurse for three hours before surrendering. Nicotine pleaded guilty to the hostage-taking and had ten months added to her parole eligibility. Defence lawyer Barry Singer warned that Nicotine would continue to be a threat unless she received intensive, long-term treatment.

"She has an actual inability to know the consequences

of her own actions," Singer said. "That's her nature. That's just the way she is."

Transferred to the women's unit of the Saskatchewan Penitentiary together, it was natural that Nicotine and Hicks joined forces once more. This time, they teamed up with two other inmates, and the four knocked down a female correctional officer, tied and blindfolded her, and dragged her into one of the cells. The inmates then spent more than four hours threatening and torturing the terrified woman, tying her to a chair and tormenting her with a broken pair of long-bladed scissors.

The inmates repeatedly punched and slapped their hostage, cut off sections of her hair and singed it with a lighter, and burned the woman's face with cigarettes. They demanded drugs, a syringe, cigarettes, food and access to a phone.

It was three years less one day since Montgomery's murder. Nicotine called the day her anniversary.

"I've already killed somebody and another one doesn't matter," she told hostage negotiators.

Nicotine advised her friends to stab the woman in the heart and throat rather than the stomach, because "those two areas are the best areas."

The incident ended when the women were promised phone calls and given fast food.

Again, Nicotine pleaded guilty, and had another three years added to her life sentence.

It was only the beginning.

In the years that followed, Nicotine was involved in several more high-profile incidents behind bars, attacking correctional officers, assaulting an inmate with a sock stuffed with soap and deodorant and tying her to a cell door and holding another prisoner hostage for an hour with a shard of glass from a broken television set.

"This isn't going to stop for Serena Nicotine," warned Bruce Moan, president of a national union of correctional officers. "Serena Nicotine can be a nice, quiet, pleasant young lady one second and the next second she can be a violent, extremely dangerous individual."

By 2001, when Nicotine attacked a guard in a shower stall at the Saskatchewan Penitentiary with a ballpoint pen, officials considered the young woman to be one of Canada's most dangerous female offenders, and said no women's prison in the country was equipped to deal with her.

"There is no place for Serena Nicotine," Moen said.

There is no place for someone who doesn't care. Someone who can't.

Parlour Tricks

FROM HIS HIDING SPOT IN THE WOODPILE, HE WATCHED THE police officer standing at the stable door. He had nothing against the man, really, but at that particular moment couldn't think of any reason not to kill him. He felt as though his brain was paralyzed, his thoughts so hazy that the only clear notion was to shoot.

So, as if compelled by some unseen force, Victor Carmel raised his hand and pulled the trigger. Then he pulled it again.

THE SEARCH FOR JAMES MCKAY JR. began on November 19, 1918, four days after the sheriff's officer left to seize several horses—or the money owing on them—from a farm east of Prince Albert. He never came back. With concern growing, Sergeant Stanley Kistruck headed out from Prince Albert in search of the missing officer, following McKay's path to the farm of Dr. Joseph Gervais.

Kistruck went with some apprehension. Like many, he was suspicious of the mysterious doctor, an eccentric French-Canadian fellow who had moved into the Steep Creek area several years earlier. There were rumours of stolen cattle, bootlegging, shady business deals. The doctor—if in fact he even was a doctor—lived in a small log cabin with two young men, a couple of teenage draft dodgers from Quebec named Victor Carmel and Jean St. Germain. The boys both wore full dark beards and moustaches, just like Gervais, and kept to themselves.

It was all a little queer.

The situation clearly didn't bode well for Officer McKay, particularly when Kistruck found traces of the missing officer's car pushed down a steep embankment into the Saskatchewan River.

A boy who lived in the area confirmed McKay's fate. He said the officer had been shot five times, his body and car pushed into the river to give the impression he had driven off the riverbank in the darkness. The boy said Dr. Gervais had forced him to help with the grim task of disposing of the evidence.

Searching the area around the doctor's cabin, Kistruck found a complex system of trenches running through the property, similar to defence trenches on a battlefield. Knowing Gervais and his boys were heavily armed with rifles, revolvers and ammunition, Kistruck went back to Prince Albert and assembled a posse to help apprehend the trio of suspects. Gervais was arrested easily at his farm, and fifteen armed men took Carmel and St. Germain two days later. They didn't go easily. Charles Horsley, a member of the posse, was ambushed and shot dead during a siege of the property.

All three of the so-called "Steep Creek bandits" were charged with murder in McKay's death—even Dr. Gervais, who was miles away when McKay was shot.

A SPECIAL HEARING TOOK PLACE in May 1919 to determine whether Gervais was sane. Though he'd shown no sign of insanity in the past, he'd tried to hang himself in jail, and his behaviour was becoming especially odd and erratic. At times during the court proceedings he would paw the air with his hands wildly and erupt into fits of convulsions. At other moments he would appear to doze off, then jolt awake and gaze frantically around the court before slumping down lifeless once more. His appearance, once so tidy and dapper, had also changed dramatically.

"He wears a long unkempt beard which, with long disheveled hair and a deathly white complexion, gives him a decidedly weird appearance," a newspaper reporter noted.

But a decidedly weird appearance was not enough to convince two doctors and a jury Gervais was insane. After less than five minutes of deliberation, he was unanimously deemed fit to stand trial for the murder of James McKay.

Gervais was tried alone, with both of his young companions testifying against him. They said Gervais had always ordered them to shoot anyone who came on his land, roaring "*Flamber la tête!*" during impassioned nightly speeches on the subject.

But that wasn't why they killed the officer. They said the doctor made them do it with the power of his mind.

GERVAIS AND ST. GERMAIN had met at a dance in St. Hyacinthe several years earlier, and within days Gervais was using the teen as a subject in his hypnotism demonstrations. Under Gervais' hypnotic spell St. Germain would feel as though his hands were glued firmly together or believe a chair was a horse, and find himself riding the chair madly as the audience screamed with laughter. Sometimes the doctor made him dance like a bear, the boy's body lumbering wildly beyond his control. At first St. Germain was hard to hypnotize but Gervais' powers grew stronger every time, until he could put the boy under with just a look.

It was the same look he used on Victor Carmel.

With Carmel it wasn't all parlour tricks. Gervais cured the boy's lung problems, soothed his nerves and strengthened his delicate health through hypnosis and magnetism. It was powerful medicine, for which Carmel was deeply grateful.

The bond between them grew deep. Gervais could soon

call the boy to him from great distances, or hide a scarf pin and transmit the hiding spot into Carmel's brain. He once hypnotized Carmel to pull a tooth, and the boy was so spellbound he didn't even flinch as it was extracted.

"He did me good to start with," Carmel said. "And he did me bad to finish with."

Bad were the thoughts Gervais put into his head, like giving the doctor all his money and moving with him to Saskatchewan, or agreeing to the secret things they would do together. Like shooting the officer standing at the stable door.

Even in court, Carmel could not escape the doctor's power.

"Dr. Gervais is still trying to hypnotize me," he cried from his spot in the witness stand. "I can feel him trying to work on me."

Gervais regarded him coolly from across the room.

St. Germain felt it too. Walking by Gervais in court, he shook the doctor's hand but seemed unable to pull his hand away. He struggled for a moment, then yanked his arm free and started crying.

"I felt as if my hand wanted to close in on the doctor's ...," he said afterward, his voice trembling. "And I gave a jerk and pulled my hand away from him as I didn't want the doctor to magnetize me."

Having abandoned his insane behaviour, Gervais remained silent and impassive throughout his trial, refusing to instruct his lawyer even when asked whether he wanted to testify in his own defence.

He had no reaction to the guilty verdict.

Carmel and St. Germain faced a jury themselves a short time later—marking the first time hypnotism was invoked as a defence in a murder trial in Canada.

The teens repeated their claims about the doctor's deadly influence, saying they had both been firmly under Gervais' spell from the time they met him in Quebec. Carmel said he was completely devoid of his own power when he saw McKay in the stable that day, and was but a slave to the murderous impulse transmitted to him by the doctor.

"So far as I am concerned it was Gervais who murdered James McKay," he said.

It almost worked.

Spanish-born hypnotist James Rodriguez, who was at the time working as a janitor at a Prince Albert apartment block, testified hypnotism can be used for good or evil, including over long distances and without the subject's consent.

David Finn, a Prince Albert lawyer involved in a society for psychic research, agreed that everything Carmel and St. Germain had described could be attributed to hypnotism. But even under the spell of a criminal hypnotist, Finn said, a right-minded person's revulsion to murder would prevent them from committing the criminal act. Their conscience would break the spell.

The jury deliberated less than half an hour.

It was an emotional moment. The jury foreman was overcome as he choked out the guilty verdicts against Carmel and St. Germain. The jury was discharged and Gervais brought into court so the three could be sentenced together.

Chief Justice Brown was also upset by the proceedings; he broke down completely while trying to pass sentence and had to adjourn for several minutes. Still fighting for his composure as he came back into court, Brown faced the three men.

"The circumstances of the crime of which you have been found guilty are so revolting that you are fortunate that the posses of police and soldiers did not shoot you on sight," he said.

Then he sentenced them to die.

"You went into hiding, you dug yourself into the ground, you conspired to defeat your country's purpose and shot down like dogs the men trying to do their duty," he said. "Under the circumstances simple justice would seem to demand that you go to the gallows in dishonour and shame."

None of the men spoke. Carmel fought back tears.

Promptly at 7:00 a.m. on October 17—eleven months after James McKay Jr. pulled his Ford into Gervais' yard—the three Steep Creek bandits walked from their cells in the Prince Albert jail and up the twenty-one steps to the scaffold. They went calmly to meet their fate, causing no trouble to the guards who accompanied them. Carmel and St. Germain prayed with a priest who walked alongside. Gervais refused last rites, but made a patriotic final statement. "The King of England stole Quebec," he shouted. "I die for my country."

The three men were hanged within one minute of the guards entering their cells.

Newspaper reporters recorded the sombre moment: "They died side by side at the same time, on the same scaffold, for the same crime."

Smoke and Mirrors

PRINCE CHARLES WATCHED CLOSELY AS THE MAN WITH THE long, dark braids and intense brown eyes manipulated the tiny pieces of bone with his hands.

The Prince of Wales was clearly taken with the entertaining demonstration. He asked questions, and appeared an eager student—to the dismay of his clock-watching handlers hovering in the Indian studies classroom of the Regina high school. But Charlie Smoke was articulate, engaging, and clearly knowledgeable about his Aboriginal culture. The teaching assistant deftly took the prince through the finer points of the Lakota hand game. Like today's shell game, it relies on sleight of hand and illusion to keep the viewer guessing.

Charlie, who often preferred his Indian name Wolf, was proud of his First Nations heritage. He revelled in its traditions, its affinity with nature and animals. He'd studied conservation biology at Oglala Lakota College and felt more comfortable with a herd of buffalo than a room full of people.

Two months after charming the prince, Charlie lamented that he hadn't made better use of the royal visit. He could have shared his thoughts on oppressive colonial governments. He might have talked about cultural genocide and racism. Or he could have pressed His Royal Highness about indigenous sovereignty.

The teacher learned to make better use of such opportunities in the future.

During his first brush with immigration authorities, Charlie threatened to go to the media with the enticing story of white men trying to kick an Indian out of Canada.

Told he'd have to leave this country if he couldn't prove his Canadian citizenship, Charlie railed in newspapers and on national television against a bureaucracy that tried to impose artificial borders on North America's First Peoples. They should be able to roam the land as freely as the deer.

Charlie explained that he was born at home thirty-nine years earlier to a Mohawk father and Lakota mother on the Akwesasne First Nation bordering Quebec, Ontario and New York State. As a result, he had no birth certificate. His parents saw no need to record the event with the government or local tribal council, he said.

Charlie's situation was further complicated by the death of his parents when he was a child, followed by the death of his grandmother when Charlie was 10. Adopted by a non-Aboriginal family, he grew up in Chicago.

Charlie insisted he was pre-Canadian, pre-American. And he wasn't leaving his home, the Aboriginal nation of Turtle Island.

"All my ancestors have been here forever," Charlie defiantly told immigration officials. "What authority does the Canadian government have to tell an indigenous person that he can't live in Canada?"

Convinced Charlie was American, immigration officers drove him to the United States border. But the US—in the high-alert environment just four months after 9/11—did not accept Smoke's gun permit as proof of his citizenship. It listed him as a member of a US Indian band

It seemed no one wanted Charlie. Except the media, which adored the story of the indigenous man without a country.

Charlie called himself a political prisoner, a resistance fighter. He likened his battle to that of Deskaheh, a chief who, eighty years earlier, could not get back in the country after addressing the League of Nations on Canadian policies against Aboriginal people.

"His last words were 'fight for the line,' meaning the imposed border through our land. And that's what I'm doing," Charlie told a national television audience.

Throughout the two-year-long battle, his wife Lisa, mother of their four young children and a Sioux Indian, remained steadfast in her support for Charlie. And soon, his plight found sympathy with politicians, First Nations leaders, and social activists. The Federation of Saskatchewan Indian Nations put its own lawyer on the case. A politician reached into his pocket to pay half of Charlie's $1,000 bail while immigration officials pressed on with their investigation.

Even when a court found Charlie guilty of using his wife's social insurance number, the judge took pity on his plight. "He asks for assistance and all he gets is prosecuted," said Justice Larry Kyle. Unable to get a social insurance number without a birth certificate, Charlie had used Lisa's number so he could work at the teaching job and provide for his family. He felt justified, not deceptive. Kyle gave him an absolute discharge

Immigration authorities were not as charitable. Charlie was kicked out of Canada.

As he stood at the Saskatchewan-North Dakota border on April 29, 2003, his 6-year-old daughter clutched a sign in her hands. "We know who our daddy is—Charlie Wolf Smoke," it read.

Canada Immigration believed they knew who he was too. But it wasn't the man calling himself Wolf Smoke, Sunkmanitu Tanka Isnala Najin, Charlie Wolfslayer, or Charlie Smoke. Fingerprints, a birth certificate and a biological father said otherwise. So did a criminal record—stretching twelve pages.

Born in Memphis, Tennessee, Charles Roger Leo Adams Jr. had been fixated on Aboriginal heritage from an early age. As a teen, he connected with a "Mountain Man" society and immersed himself in Native history and culture. Charlie grew his hair long and called himself Leo Wolfslayer.

His father may have actually had a tiny bit of Iroquois blood in his veins, but not enough to satisfy Charlie. In 1981, he broke with his white family. At the Pine Ridge Reservation, Charlie met an elderly Oglala Sioux Tribal member—the real Charlie Smoke. When the old man died, Charlie wanted to be Indian so badly, he appropriated the name.

Four years after Charlie had played hand games with the Prince of Wales, an Oglala Sioux Tribal Court judge agreed Smoke, the Indian, was really Adams, the white man.

While Charlie likens himself to other Indian exiles, he disagrees with a more damning comparison.

In 1937, Prince Charles's mother and his aunt—then the young Princesses Elizabeth and Margaret—were enthralled with the buckskin-clad man with braids who had come to Buckingham Palace. Aboriginal writer and lecturer Grey Owl found in Princess Elizabeth an eager student as she listened to his stories of the Canadian wilderness.

Like Charlie Smoke, Englishman Archie Belaney, who was also raised by his grandmother, had a keen interest in nature and American Indians as a child. When he came to Canada, he satisfied both his passions. Archie became the Ojibway Indian Grey Owl. Only after his death was his fraud exposed.

From his place of exile or homeland—depending who or what you believe—Charlie still plays his guessing games.

"I have to do what I have to for the sake of my children," he wrote on one of his Web sites in 2006. "Believe what you will. That is not my concern anymore." The statement was posted a day after "Charlie Smoke" pleaded guilty in a South Dakota courtroom to false impersonation.

The Mayor's Daughter

THE RINGING TELEPHONE BROKE THE SILENCE OF WHAT HAD been a typically quiet Sunday afternoon.

"Estevan City Police," the lone officer answered. "Sergeant Dupré."

"Ray, my boyfriend has just committed suicide," came the response. The female voice was so calm, considering the words being spoken, that Sergeant Ray Dupré initially thought the call a hoax.

"Who's calling?" he asked. It was Dawn Kickley. Dupré recognized the woman as a friend of his children. She gave her address.

"Tell them to hurry," she said and hung up.

Dupré interrupted lunch for two constables sitting at the popular Estevan Bowl, better known to most locals as simply "E.B.s." Greg Baxter worked there as a cook and waiter. He had just gotten off shift about twelve hours earlier.

Baxter, the big-city Montreal boy, had met Kickley, a small-town Saskatchewan girl—daughter of the mayor of Lampman—at a ski resort in Banff. He was a cook in the staff cafeteria. Kickley, who had quit high school at 16 to wait tables at a local truck stop, was a chambermaid. When she became pregnant, the lovers left the mountains for the Prairies, moving to Estevan near Kickley's family.

Now, six months later on October 22, 1989, Kickley's mostly nude body was covered head to toe in Baxter's blood when she met the two constables at the door.

"This is just too weird. Greg, why did you do this?" she rambled on frantically.

The police officer pulled a blanket off the couch to wrap around the shaking, pathetic 20-year-old, only to find his partner had already draped a jacket over her shoulders. Kickley reached for a cigarette to calm her nerves.

Inside the master bedroom, Constable Greg Catley found Baxter laid out on the bed, his feet where his head would normally lie. He was naked, but the cook had apparently died with a large black-handled butcher knife clutched in his right hand, lying on his chest. The blade was now pointed at his feet, but it had punctured his heart. The wound was in the shape of an inverted L, like someone had given the knife a twist.

What Catley had not expected to find at this suicide call was the tiny body lying next to her 25-year-old father. Baby Amanda's open sleeper revealed a wound that went from stem to stern, allowing her intestines to protrude. The knife had even gone clear through, exiting out her back. Amanda was only twenty days old. Catley assumed both father and daughter were dead and went to tell his partner. But when he stepped back into the bedroom, the constable noticed Amanda's legs kick. She was breathing.

The infant returned by ambulance to the same Estevan hospital where she had entered the world less than three weeks earlier. Within hours, she too was dead.

By contrast, her mother had just three superficial wounds to her left breast. A doctor put in a few stitches.

And then Kickley started to weave her tale.

Lying on the couch after breast-feeding her fussy infant, she awoke to a sharp pain in her chest. Kickley thought she was having a heart attack. But Baxter, moody and sullen at being passed over for a job in Vancouver, was standing over her with a knife. "Greg was freaking out,"

Kickley told police, family and friends. She got up from the couch and found her baby wounded and her boyfriend dead with knife in hand.

There was only one problem with Kickley's story. Would a dead man have removed a knife from his chest?

Kickley pulled a few more threads from her memory. Now Baxter was not dead when she went into the bedroom. Rather, he was threatening to kill himself. They struggled. She fell on him, plunging the knife into his chest. She pulled the weapon out, and left it in his hand.

But that was not quite right either, it seems. Police tried to re-enact what Kickley had described and found it implausible.

So she gave her story another twist.

After Kickley awoke, she ran to the bedroom because she heard Amanda crying, she said. Baxter, who had fought with Kickley's sister a couple weeks earlier, was standing over the baby with a knife dripping blood. "Your life isn't worth living," he shouted. Kickley demanded to know what he had done to the baby. She ran at him, they struggled over the knife, fell on the bed, struggled some more, and the knife entered Baxter's body. She pulled the knife out, and left it on Baxter's chest while she went to her child. That would explain how she transferred Baxter's blood to the baby's pink crib sheet.

On further reflection, Kickley spun another version. When she walked into the bedroom, Baxter was holding the knife to his chest with both hands. "Our lives aren't worth living," he said. They struggled. He fell on the bed. She fell on top, and the knife went into him. She pulled the knife out and put pressure on the wound. Her nursing bra, which had no cuts or holes despite the wounds to her breast, was so heavy with blood, she took it off and dropped it on the bed. Investigators found it beneath Baxter's arm.

At her trial, Kickley's story started to unravel.

She had not fallen on Baxter, rather they had fallen

together. "I remember getting up and realized that he was stabbed." She heard a clunking noise, but didn't actually see the knife enter her boyfriend's chest. And having pulled out the knife, she washed the weapon and her hands, then placed the knife back on his chest. Somehow in those motions, she must have stabbed herself, because there was now blood on the knife's blade. That's why the knife only had her blood on it and to the same depth as the wounds to her breast. She pushed or pulled his body around—which would explain the blood stains at the head of the bed—and placed her lips over his. She gave some life-saving breaths, but to no avail.

"I know I didn't fall on that knife," she said. "I may have said that to everyone. But it is not true."

Clearly, the jury did not think this was the only deception. Despite Kickley's tangled tale, she was convicted of second-degree murder.

After Kickley appealed, the prosecution argued: "It is a classic example of someone caught in a web of her own lies."

But the pretty, young killer also caught someone else in her net—an ambulance attendant. They met at the murder scene, and their courtship continued even after Kickley was convicted. With her appeal pending and Kickley out on bail, they became engaged. Writing to a fellow inmate, Kickley even spoke of having another child. But the engagement was broken off after her bail was revoked—when Kickley had been caught handling a gun in a Lampman park.

In 2000, the woman who had been convicted of killing her boyfriend and twenty-day-old child was helping to raise baby birds behind bars for a wildlife rehabilitation program.

"I think every prison should have baby birds," Kickley said when interviewed in prison by an Edmonton newspaper reporter. "Everyone has a love for animals."

Unforgotten

HE ALWAYS STRUCK EARLY IN THE MORNING, JUST BEFORE THE sun had started to rise, and the women had not. He didn't know them, but he knew a lot about their neighbourhood—that the low-rent townhouses were filled with women living alone or with their children. A petty thief who was first caught stealing at age 12 when he shoplifted a baseball glove, he grew into a man with a low, menacing voice who used a screwdriver to jimmy doors on the homes he broke into. The curly-headed bandit with the masked face would find women in their beds—and take what he wanted. Though his crimes had moved far beyond petty, sometimes he still couldn't resist pocketing a few dollars after stealing his victims' sense of security.

Between 1983 and 1984, the crimes in Regina's Glencairn area went from isolated incidents to establishing a disturbing, calculated pattern. There were at least seven similar attacks in 1984 alone. It was June that year when officers watched for the Glencairn Rapist to make his appearance at the townhouses in the city's east side. Constable Marv Taylor was among the police officers lying in wait. And he waited in vain.

The rapist and thief slipped away—and out of his reach.

THE INTRUDER WAS SEEN RUNNING from a townhouse around 6:30 a.m. where he had pried open the front door with a screwdriver. It was one of five homes in the same complex burglarized that morning on December 1, 1984. Police followed tracks in the snow and found Larry Clare Deckert crouched behind a television set in another house just a few doors down. Inside his pocket was a rubber mask. "I don't want no one to see me if they already know me," was the only explanation he offered.

A search of Deckert's house, only three blocks from the townhouses, produced a photo album of him growing up. Tucked in the back was a newspaper clipping circled in heavy, dark ink. It told of an 18-year-old who had been arrested in July and charged with four of the Glencairn rapes.

Some cops were struck by Deckert's resemblance to a sketch of the Glencairn Rapist. But by then, the teen accused of the crimes was sitting in jail, awaiting his trial.

Meanwhile, Deckert cut a deal. He admitted to burglarizing four of the townhouses, and the Crown dropped a fifth charge. A month before Deckert's arrest, a masked man had attacked a twelve-year-old girl in her Glencairn townhouse while she slept on a couch. The intruder forced the girl to perform oral sex, but was interrupted when the victim's father came home. The two men struggled, and the intruder got away. Unable to prove the attacker's identity, the Crown withdrew that charge against Deckert.

The tall, lanky teen accused of being the Glencairn Rapist went on trial in February 1985, but the case ended abruptly on Valentine's Day. Prosecutors decided they didn't have any solid evidence, and he was set free after spending seven months behind bars.

By then, Deckert was already safely serving his six-month jail sentence for the break-ins.

TWO YEARS LATER, A YOUNG clerk named Julie was working the night shift alone at a convenience store when she was attacked by a robber wielding a hockey stick and wearing what passed for a goalie's mask. He pushed Julie into a back room, tugged her pants down and ripped off her panties and bra. Needing something with which to bind her ankles and wrists, the robber yanked an extension cord from the wall.

"How would you like something else," he said, waving the tip of the extension cord, his hands groping at Julie's body. But he never delivered on his ugly threat, as the frightened, 22-year-old clerk begged him: "Please don't. I'm pregnant!"

The attacker hit Julie in the face and fled, taking with him the cash from the register, some cigarettes, and a bit of money from Julie's purse. "Don't move, bitch," he said repeatedly, "or you're dead."

Within minutes of Julie untying herself, police had the store surrounded. Nearby, officers found a stalled pick-up truck containing the robber's loot, a hockey stick and a make-shift hockey mask. Deckert emerged from behind some apartments and was arrested.

Back at the police station, the mask tweaked memories. A victim of the Glencairn Rapist had described her attacker as wearing a homemade, padded, brown leather mask with stitching, not unlike the masks worn by goaltenders in hockey. Still, Deckert denied any involvement, and so the Glencairn rapes went unsolved.

TANYA HAD SHOWERED OFF the dust from a late night at the 1989 Big Valley Jamboree, and now, as the sun was rising, she put down the book she was reading, turned off the lamp, and fell asleep.

She had been in bed for only an hour when she awoke, sensing someone was in her second-floor suite. That July night was the only time she had left the glass balcony door open, ever so slightly, in hopes of allowing a breeze inside. Instead, an intruder had widened the gap with a jackknife and slipped into the apartment. A towel covering his head, he put an arm around Tanya's neck. He had a knife, he told her, and Tanya could indeed feel something pressing into her neck. "Keep quiet," said a low, gravelly voice, "or I'll kill you."

Straddling her on her bed, the intruder unzipped his pants, forced up her night shirt, and pushed her legs apart. But, unlike the others, this attack would not go his way.

Tanya clamped her teeth down tightly on a ring finger and directed a few blows at the intruder's groin. "Fucking bitch," he said, rewarding her bravery with a barrage of punches that blackened Tanya's eyes. The intruder then fled, leaving blood on the sheets, not all of it Tanya's.

At the police station that same day, Sergeant Marv Taylor had a hunch about who the intruder might be. The early-morning break-in, the knife, a masked face—it all fit a disturbing pattern Taylor had not forgotten since the stake-out five years earlier.

Deckert had been granted parole midway into a four-year prison sentence. He was back in Regina, staying at a downtown halfway house, but had been free that week-end on a pass.

Taylor found Deckert on a job site. When the suspect removed his work gloves, the cop immediately noticed the ring finger on Deckert's right hand was bandaged. "I banged it this morning," Deckert said, but Taylor wouldn't buy it. Tanya's address book, ripped to pieces, was found at the home of Deckert's parents, where he had spent the weekend. Deckert had attacked Tanya only forty-one days into his parole for the crimes involving Julie.

TAYLOR CAREFULLY TOOK THE bandage covering Deckert's wound as evidence, as were the blood stains collected from Tanya's apartment. Not only would they link Deckert to the attack on Tanya, but Taylor—still haunted by spectre of the Glencairn Rapist—hoped for more. Police now had DNA testing in their forensic arsenal. Taylor went looking for the rape kits from the Glencairn cases—only to learn they had been ordered destroyed after the charges against the teen had fallen apart. The cop known for his determination was undeterred.

Deep in the property office, he discovered two rape kits had slipped through the procedural cracks. Elated, Taylor believed he was on the brink of catching the Glencairn Rapist. He hoped DNA culled from the rape kits could be compared with samples of blood left by Deckert on Tanya's sheets. The blood stains did make it to the RCMP lab, but the tests were not considered a priority, as Deckert himself wouldn't be going anywhere anytime soon. In May 1990, he was sentenced to five years in prison for aggravated sexual assault on Tanya, and an additional two years for breaking into another home that same weekend.

The DNA testing never was done. The blood stains disappeared from the RCMP crime lab, as did Deckert's bloody bandage. Taylor boxed up his files and pushed them under his desk, taking solace in the fact Deckert would remain behind bars for a while. The veteran vice cop moved on, but not before he asked a fellow officer to let him know when Deckert would be released.

TAYLOR, BY THEN THE OFFICER in charge of fraud investigations, got the call in December 1997. The following month, he pulled out the boxes he had tucked away. He couldn't forget what he had read in those files.

"It's terrifying," he says. "You empathize with the victims. You think of the fear they went through. I figured something had to be done."

Taylor had asked Deckert back in 1989 to voluntarily provide a blood sample, and Deckert had refused. "I told him then the cases would come back to haunt him." Indeed, the passage of time had worked to Taylor's advantage. DNA testing had improved, and the law also caught up, making it possible to require suspects to provide blood and hair for testing. Samples taken from Deckert, who was still in an Ontario prison, were compared with the two rape kits Taylor had rescued.

A SINGLE MOTHER OF TWO, Jane had been asleep in her Glencairn townhouse in April 1984 when she heard the creaking of a door early in the morning. In the light from the hallway, she saw the silhouette of a man wearing a white ski mask. He was armed with a knife, and he threatened to kill her if she wasn't quiet. He put a sock in her mouth, and then raped her.

Two years later, in the same housing complex, Anne, a single woman who lived alone with two children, was attacked around five in the morning. Sobbing, Anne begged to be left in peace. Instead, the intruder slashed her forehead and had his way, telling the woman, "If you don't cooperate, I'll slit you wide open." He swiped a few dollars from her dresser before he left.

When Deckert's genetic profile was compared with that of the rapist who had attacked Jane and Anne, it was a perfect match.

The two rape kits that had fallen between the cracks ensured Deckert would not.

"It was kind of a nice feeling, after all these years, to bring closure," recalls Taylor.

Deckert was due to leave Warkworth prison on May 11, 1998, a free man. Thanks to Taylor's diligence, however, he was charged that very day with the attacks on Jane and Anne. "It would have been nice to have the (rape) kits from all the others," Taylor laments. But in the end, it would not matter.

Deckert pleaded guilty only to sexually assaulting Anne. It was one of the "callous, brutal and senseless" crimes Justice Ron Barclay took into consideration when 37-year-old Deckert was declared a dangerous offender, meaning he will remain in prison until he's no longer a risk to society.

During the hearing, Anne, Julie and Tanya each took her turn in the witness box, reliving the horror they experienced years earlier at his hands. The passing of time had not dulled their memories, or their fear of the thief who stole their right to feel safe in their beds.

Tanya would never sleep in her apartment again. She even got rid of her bed; and while she replaced it with a new one, rarely does she actually sleep in it. Tanya favours the couch, where she dozes beside her dogs as they keep watch.

Anne, Julie and Tanya are pseudonyms. A court order prohibits publication of any information which would identify them.

The Painting

Slowly he dipped the brush into the paint and drew it across the paper.

This painting was large, two feet wide and nearly as long, and he'd been working on it for weeks. With great care he filled in the green background with his one small, frayed brush, then carefully added gold lettering that spelled out a special Christmas message wishing health, wealth and happiness. At the top of the page he had painted a guard in a blue coat shooting red arrows into the green expanse.

Bill Kurulak had done many paintings, but this was to be his last.

It was a wet July night when Bill and his teenaged brother, Mike, piled into a stolen blue Plymouth with their friend Bill Miller, heading from the Kurulak family farm near Canora to Saskatoon.

The two Bills had met in prison several months earlier while the 24-year-old Kurulak was serving time for stealing furs, and the 37-year-old Miller was in for a series of thefts and frauds.

The men hooked up again on the outside, and had been spending the summer of 1932 romping around the Saskatchewan countryside together, sometimes with 17-

year-old Mike in tow. The trio was finding all sorts of trouble that summer, breaking into gas stations, stealing gas and oil, robbing stores of jewellery, clothes, hardware, guns and ammunition.

Porter McLeod knew the men were up to something when they came into the Fort Qu'Appelle hardware store where he worked one June afternoon. McLeod was particularly unimpressed with Miller, a rough man with a hard mug topped by an unruly tussle of curls.

"If you're not just out of jail you haven't been out long," McLeod thought to himself as he looked at Miller.

When the store was broken into that night, McLeod knew immediately who the culprits were.

The trio pulled off another break-in in Theodore three days later, and then another a few days after that, taking thousands of dollars worth of guns, ammunition, tools and clothes.

They were stealing so much they couldn't even get rid of all of it, particularly the clothes. The Kurulaks had offered suits and dresses to their brother and sister, but their law-abiding siblings had refused to take the stolen property. So on that rainy July night, the trio of thieves packed up three bags of stolen clothes, and headed off in the Plymouth to see if they could find any buyers.

A police officer standing on the road in a rain slicker changed their plan. When the men didn't stop for the officer a wild chase ensued, with Miller shooting out through the back window, and both cars careening through the countryside mile after mile. The officer pulled off the road in Sheho, telephoning another officer in Foam Lake to pick up the chase.

Winnipeg salesman A.E. Wells was sleeping at a roadside camp near Foam Lake when he was jolted awake by the sound of a car speeding by at 3:00 a.m. Wells heard five loud explosions, then another, then three more. He thought it was a car backfiring at first, but looking outside he knew it wasn't. He saw three men standing around an

RCMP car, then heard more shots. As the men sped away in another vehicle, Wells heard a cry.

"Sandy," a man was calling. "Help."

Wells and Lorne "Sandy" Baird, a railway employee who lived nearby, ran to the car and found an RCMP officer bleeding from the chest.

"They've got me," Corporal Leonard Ralls said. "They've gone east."

With the ignition wiring ripped out of the RCMP car, Baird put the injured man in his own vehicle and sped toward town. The injured 44-year-old officer seemed better as they approached the doctor's house, but then he begun to gasp.

"It is too late," he said. "I am finished."

He was. The search for his killers, however, had just began.

News of the murdered officer spread quickly. Nearly forty RCMP officers were assigned to the manhunt, and a few hundred civilians joined posses to help with the pursuit. It was a gruelling task. There were few roads in the area, and they were soggy and nearly impassable. Rough land, dense wood and deep sloughs took their toll on police and civilians alike, as they searched for days without sleep, food or reprieve from the relentless pursuit. With no phone service, police communicated with the posses through written messages dropped from a plane.

Two days after the shooting, the RCMP inspector leading the search promised the bandits would be brought to justice.

"I'll not sleep until I get these murderers," he vowed.

Slowly the net tightened.

Mike Kurulak was the first to be caught, taken by a posse while guarding the trio's stolen horses northeast of Kelvington. He was arrested easily, and soon gave up the names of his cohorts.

Dominion jail warden W.J. Macleod was not surprised to hear one of the wanted men was Bill Miller.

"He would shoot in a minute," Macleod said. "Killing Ralls is just the sort of trick he would be up to."

Bill Kurulak was surrounded by four police officers and a civilian while he slept upstairs in a Kelvington-area house the next morning. Miller was the last to go, chased into a clump of bushes by police that night. There was a brief gun battle, but as the posse closed in Miller put the gun to his right temple and pulled the trigger, fulfilling his vow that he would never be taken alive. He died clutching his revolver.

A divinity student brought news of Miller's death into Kelvington, screeching into town in a car that had been battered by the punishing search. Three doors had been torn from the vehicle, and there was only one fender and no bumper. It was, according to newspaper accounts, "the worst-looking wreck that ever reached here under its own power."

The searchers and suspects didn't look much better; they pulled into town mud-caked, bloodied and exhausted from the brutal hunt. The search had lasted four days, cost thousands of dollars, and caused serious damage to at least forty cars. It was the biggest and most dramatic manhunt in the province's history.

Despite the Kurulaks' assertion that Miller alone had shot Ralls, a jury found both brothers guilty in the officer's death. Mike Kurulak was sentenced to fifteen years in prison for manslaughter. His older brother Bill was sentenced to hang for murder.

BILL KURULAK DIDN'T SLEEP AT ALL. He prayed and wrote letters to his sister, his brother, and his parents. He ate breakfast at three in the morning, or tried to, anyway. It was bacon, eggs, toast and coffee—a good breakfast, but he could stomach little of it, picking at the meal until he gave up in favour of cigarettes.

He was smoking when they came for him. It was 6:00 a.m., still dark, when the guards took him, pinning his arms behind his back and leading him outside. They walked a short distance, and then up some steps.

The hangman slipped a black cap over Kurulak's head, and pulled the inch-thick rope, with its perfect and dreadful knot, around his slender neck. There was the Lord's Prayer, and the trap dropped.

Bill Kurulak died with a half smile on his face, silently, without saying a word.

Jail officials were impressed at how quietly and bravely he met his death, and said he was one of the coolest men to ever be executed at the Regina jail.

His final painting was hung too—in a wooden frame, above the warden's desk.

Worlds Apart

THE RAIN THAT HAD BEEN FALLING MOST OF THE DAY WAS making for a cool, quiet night as Charlene Rosebluff stood in the street light's glow. Near the downtown bars and hotels, but not too far from home, this was where Charlene worked. It was known as the low stroll, because the mostly poor, often drug-addicted Aboriginal women didn't charge more than $60. Sometimes, when they were particularly desperate, the price dropped lower. Only 21 years old, Charlene, a petite, pretty woman with dark, tired eyes, was a veteran. She had stood on these street corners since she was barely a teenager.

Charlene had been waiting about half an hour when the white, four-door car stopped beside her. From the open window, she heard a man ask if she wanted to go with them. Both knew what he was really asking. Charlene leaned into the window to negotiate, but almost immediately took a step back. She could smell the booze and quickly sized up the situation: two to one. "You guys are too young, and you guys are drunk."

They didn't appreciate the brush off. Bitch, slut, Indian trash, she heard. "That's why nobody will go with you," Charlene muttered as the white Honda Accord sped away.

She turned down a side street, and Charlene saw the same car stopped in an alley.

The sandy-haired driver climbed into the trunk. The passenger with the dark, curly hair jumped into the driver's seat and steered the car around the block, stopping in front of Charlene again. And again, she turned them away. "I know you guys are up to no good."

"Fucking squaw," came the response. Street-tough Charlene liked to believe the words meant nothing to her. But she would remember them long afterwards.

She saw the car again, driving without its headlights on. It pulled up beside her. Did they think she was stupid? They had to know who she was, Charlene thought to herself. The original driver was back at the wheel. He offered her $60, but Charlene turned it down. She couldn't see the other guy, but felt certain he was in the trunk. And while Charlene got into strangers' cars regularly, nothing about this felt right.

Charlene's nickname was Spiderwoman. She could pick up on things—with her so-called "spidey sense."

LENNY HALL STOLE A BICYCLE to search for his girlfriend when she didn't come home that night. It was not without some difficulty that he manoeuvred through the wet, downtown streets. Lenny was nursing a couple of broken ribs. He had last seen Pamela George shortly after midnight when they had shared a cigarette, passing it back and forth through an open window in their apartment. Welfare paid the rent. Lenny had been inside, perched on a dresser. Pam, still outside, had been getting ready to leave again. The regular who had dropped her off had no money. After the cigarette, Pam had walked off into the night to try to find someone who did.

Lenny gave up looking around 6:30 in the morning. The bicycle he had stolen to aid his search was later stolen from him.

That same morning, Alexander Ternowetsky paid $120 cash for a ticket from Regina to Calgary. He was going to meet friends in Banff on a ski trip. After dropping his buddy off at the Regina airport, Steven Kummerfield drove his father's white, four-door Honda Accord to the car wash. He cleaned it inside and out.

If Alex had bothered to look out the airplane's window after take-off, he would have noticed the police cars stopped on a grid road west of the airport. He might have made out a yellow sheet. It was the kind used to cover up a body at a crime scene.

A GOVERNMENT WORKER TAKING a back-country road to work early in the morning was the first to spot her. Pam lay face down near a slough on a stubble field. The zipper on her mud-caked jeans was open and her sweater and light jacket were hiked up, exposing her back. Two condoms were all her pockets held.

Police suspected Pam's boyfriend or maybe a former pimp or a drug-dealer. They were not looking for two clean-cut, university students, who had enjoyed every opportunity in life—unlike Pam.

The firstborn of young parents struggling with poverty and alcoholism, Pam was close to her grandmother who helped raise her on the Sakimay First Nation. As a teen, she loved to read romance novels, always longing for someone and something more from life. Both eluded her. Sixteen years old with only her Grade 9, Pam moved to Regina where she found abusive partners and further despair. She buried a son six years before her own death. The 2-year-old, her second child, drowned in a dugout on the reserve. With few skills, little education, and a welfare cheque that never stretched far enough, Pam struggled to raise her two daughters. Her children occasionally ended up in the care of family members, just as she had. Much like the books she read as a girl, Pam looked for an escape. She found it in the "poor man's heroin"—pills crushed and watered down—that she shot into her arms. Occasionally, she stepped out on a street corner to get the money she needed.

Alex started his Easter weekend in Regina with about $370 in his pocket, and made several more withdrawals from his account before he left for Banff. The son of a university professor, he had grown up in Regina but had moved a year earlier to Prince George, BC, and had just finished his first year of university. He wanted to spend Easter weekend partying with his friends before starting a tree planting job in BC the following month. Alex and Steve had known each other since high school. A promising basketball player with the University of Regina Cougars, Steve was in his first year of studies with plans to become a Phys. Ed teacher.

Steve had taken his girlfriend out for supper on April 17, 1995, and was back home when Alex phoned around 9:30 p.m. They agreed to meet at a place they called Rainbow Bridge—so named because of the way the concrete sides arced. The secluded spot near the Wascana Golf and Country Club was a good place to hang out and drink. It was also walking distance from Steve's home in the suburbs. He hadn't been waiting long when a taxi pulled up. "Allie?" he shouted into the darkness. "Stevie!" came the reply. Two buddies and a "40" of Southern Comfort.

STEVE AND ALEX KNEW NOTHING of Pam George's life. But they knew a lot about her death.

Sitting in a hot tub in Banff with a friend hours after leaving Regina, the story Alex told about how he spent his Easter weekend spilled out. He and Steve had been out drinking when they decided to try picking up a hooker, but she wouldn't go with both of them. Alex hid in the trunk. When the car stopped near the airport, he climbed out. Alex thought she was scared because she asked them to let her go. She gave Steve oral sex, then Alex took a turn. Steve started to hit her; Alex hit Steve; and then together they hit the woman. "We both lost it," Alex told his friend and showed him a cut on his knuckle. They left her at the side of the road and drove away, without paying her. Alex said if he ever got caught, he would take off for Australia.

Around the same time Alex was chatting in the hot tub, Steve was also talking. His friend phoned and asked what he and Alex had done the night before. "Not much," said Steve. "We drove around, got drunk, and killed this chick."

Steve said they had picked up some triple-X beer and a hooker. They drove to the "Alport"—a spot where Alex liked to drink near the airport. His friend would later remember Steve saying the woman tried to run when Alex got out of the trunk. Steve got a blow job. Alex was in the car with her when Steve got mad and wanted to leave. He tried to grab Alex from the car, but Alex wanted to let her finish. They beat her. Steve said she was screaming at them as they drove away.

They stopped in White City for hamburgers, before spending what was left of the night at a lakefront cabin owned by Steve's grandfather. That's where they woke up the next morning, looked at each other, and said, "What the hell did we do?'" Steve recalled.

Several other friends also heard pieces of the story. They didn't tell the police, who had questioned Pam's former boyfriend four times. "You're barking up the wrong tree," he told the cops, adding they should be looking for a trick gone bad. Investigators didn't start looking for Steve and Alex until someone overheard the friends talking and went to the police three weeks after Pam's body was discovered.

After the pair's arrest in May 1995, Dave Cote took Alex into the exercise yard at the Regina jail—a half-hour reprieve from being locked up for twenty-three and half hours a day. The white men awaiting trial for killing the Saulteaux woman had to be kept in protective custody in jail where the racial mix is opposite what it is outside.

The inmate and the guard chatted about high school sports, but there was no escaping the obvious. "You fellas got yourselves into a bit of a mess," said Cote. "Yes, it's so confusing," Alex replied. He talked about Australia. He had been born there and had dual citizenship. He would start over again in the country of his birth some day—when he got out.

Cote and Alex talked again a few days later after the inmate's failed attempt at bail. The nineteen-year-old was worried about serving a life sentence behind bars. "Twenty-five years is a long time," said Alex.

INA GEORGE SITS IN THE HALLWAY, listening as footsteps echo on the slate floors. She is waiting for the ones that will let her know the jury has reached a verdict. Her slight frame and quiet ways shouldn't be mistaken for frailty. There is an iron resolve that brings this 56-year-old mother, grandmother and great-grandmother to the courtroom each day. She needs to be here; needs to pay homage to her dead child—just as she did a decade before.

Her son Chad was 33 years old when he joined his older sister Pam in death. About to become a father for the fifth time, he had been hoping to make a new start with his life. Instead, he found himself in an inner-city drug house, where he was brutally beaten by an addict. Ina was working in the band office on Sakimay when she got the call that another of her children had fallen victim to a lifestyle that brought them to harm. Street life was dangerous. But that didn't make their lives any less valued. Ina loved her children unconditionally, just as they loved her. The tattoo on Pam's arm had read "I love mom."

Waiting to learn the fate of her son's killer in 2005, Ina couldn't escape the memory of Pam's death had she tried. Chad's killer sat in the same prisoner box from which Alex and Steve had once faced their jury. Steve's lawyer was now the judge, presiding over the trial of Daniel Alvin Brass, the man who had beaten Chad to death with a beach umbrella. Charlene Rosebluff, who overheard Brass in an argument the next day, was again a reluctant witness. And for Ina, there was the same wrenching mix of anger and hurt. This time, the throngs of media and protesters stayed home.

"These two university students coming from a high class family and us, we're way down here—that got a lot of attention from everybody," Ina told a lone reporter.

Sadly, one poor, Aboriginal man killing another was a story told too many times.

Nine years had passed since Steve and Alex were sent to prison for killing Pam. Back then, 10-year-old Chelsea, Pam's eldest daughter, had worn a little button with her mother's picture on it as she sat next to Ina during the trial. Chelsea was now a young mother herself when Ina learned Chad's killer, convicted of second-degree murder, was sentenced to life with no chance to seek parole for ten years.

A couple of weeks after testifying against Chad's murderer, the woman whose "spidey sense" likely spared her life on April 17, 1995, died in a hotel room. Charlene's death was blamed on a drug overdose, not the desperation that drove her to stick a needle in her arm or get into a car with strangers for money.

THE SAME YEAR INA WAITED in that hallway to learn the fate of her son's killer, Alex graduated from university with a master's of arts in editing and publishing. He took a job at a newspaper, edited a lifestyle magazine aimed at rich tourists, and revelled in writing about his travels. His co-workers knew him as a likable guy, although he tended to get into scrapes when he drank. And he did. A drunken row in a hotel found him in a courtroom again. It probably wouldn't have made headlines, except by then Alex had invested $29,000 in a newspaper, making him part-owner and managing editor. He was fined and told to stay out of trouble.

Back in the courtyard at the Regina jail, Alex had feared he was facing at least twenty-five years of his life in prison. But Alex and Steve were convicted of manslaughter, not murder. Paroled in 2000, their sentences expired three years later. Just as he had once vowed, Alex ran away to Australia, a country once used as a penal colony. There he earned his degree, bought into a newspaper business, and started over.

On a University of Melbourne website for his graduating class, a tanned, fit-looking, youthful Alex smiles in a photograph above an update on his career. "Butchers aren't the only people with blood on their hands in Rockhampton," he says of his new home. "And this makes Rocky a very lively place to report the daily news."

Sources and Reference Material

Grocery Misconduct
Court transcripts and documents; *Regina Leader-Post*.

A Good and Faithful Servant
Moosomin *The World*; Regina *Morning Leader*; *Regina Leader-Post*; *Winnipeg Free Press*; National Archives file; "The John Morrison Story" from *Outlaws of Saskatchewan* by Frank W. Anderson, Gopher Books.

Room 104
Court transcripts and documents; *Regina Leader-Post*; *National Post*.

The Long Ride
Al Lyon's scrapbook courtesy of the Lyon family; police documents; *Daniels County Leader*; *Regina Leader-Post*.

Dreams and Nightmares
Court transcripts and documents; *Regina Leader-Post*; Canadian Press; *Saskatoon StarPhoenix*; *Edmonton Journal*; *Calgary Herald*.

Gold Watches and White Collars
Court transcripts and documents; National Parole Board decisions; *Saskatoon StarPhoenix*; *Victoria Times-Columnist*; Innovation Place Newsletter September 2001 Edition.

Spotless to the End
Regina *Morning Leader*; *The Last Dance: Murder in Canada* by Neil Boyd, Prentice-Hall Canada Inc., 1988; National Archives file.

The Hold-Up
Court transcripts and documents; *Prince Albert Daily Herald*; Canadian Press.

Brown Fall
Court transcripts and documents; *Regina Leader-Post*; Canadian Press; *Moose Jaw Times Herald*.

An Area of Insanity
Regina Leader-Post; *Moncton Times Transcript*; *Windsor Star*; Canadian Press; *Winnipeg Free Press*; "The Guy Who Bugs Our Anne" by E. Kaye Fulton, *The Toronto Star*, November 3, 1985; *Snowbird: The Story of Anne Murray* by Barry Grills, Quarry Press, 1996.

Loyalty, Trust and Truthfulness
Court transcripts, documents and evidence videos; *Saskatoon StarPhoenix*.

The Boy Who Wanted To Fly
Court transcripts and documents, including agreed statement of facts, written judgment and psychiatric report; *Saskatoon StarPhoenix*; *Edmonton Journal*; Canadian Press.

Blood Relatives
Court transcripts and documents; *Regina Leader-Post*.

A Snake Around His Heart
National Archives file; Regina *Morning Leader*; *The Saskatoon Phoenix*; *Prince Albert Daily Herald*; *The History of the Oleskiw Family* by Shirley Oleskiw, 1998; national census documents for 1901, 1906, 1911.

Whiter Than Mine
Court transcripts and documents; *Regina Leader-Post*; *Saskatoon StarPhoenix*; *Medicine Hat News*; *Edmonton Journal*; *Weyburn Review*; Canadian Press.

Top Dog
Regina Leader-Post; *Saskatoon StarPhoenix*; *The Globe and Mail*; Fort Qu'Appelle *Times*.

The Hunter and the Hunted
Regina Leader-Post; *Saskatoon StarPhoenix*; *Just Another Indian: A Serial Killer and Canada's Indifference* by Warren Goulding, Fifth House Ltd., 2001.

Friendly Fire
Court transcripts and documents; *Regina Leader-Post*; *Toronto Star*.

Football, Fowl Suppers and Funerals
Court transcripts and documents; *Regina Leader-Post*.

Of Death and Survival
Reporter's notes; *Regina Leader-Post*; interviews; court documents.

Art and Avarice
Regina Leader-Post; *The Globe and Mail*; reporter's notes; *Saskatchewan Reports* (4 Sask. R., p. 64)

Sour Milk
Regina Leader-Post; National Archives file; "The Case of the Missing Farmer" from *Outlaws of Saskatchewan* by Frank W. Anderson, Gopher Books.

Dr. John and Mr. Schneeberger
Court transcripts and documents; *Regina Leader Post*; *Calgary Herald*; "Justice for Candice" by Robert Kiener from *Reader's Digest*, July 2004; reporter's notes.

Copycat
Court transcripts and documents; *Regina Leader-Post*.

Dining With Daniel
Court documents; *Regina Leader-Post*; reporter's notes.

The Truth About Carney
Regina Leader-Post; *The Globe and Mail*; *Edmonton Journal*; Canadian Press; Report of the Commission of Inquiry into the Shooting Death of Leo LaChance; *Buried in the Silence* by Connie Samson, NeWest Press, 1995.

Hollywood Ending
Court transcripts and documents; *Regina Leader-Post*.

The Power of Persuasion
Regina Leader-Post; *National Post*; Canadian Press; *The Carillon*; University of Regina press releases; court documents; Annual Report of the Teaching Development Centre, University of Regina; Review of the Nguyen Case at the University of Regina, May 17, 2001 by Stuart McKinnon and Constance Rooke; Website: http://members.fortunecity.com/nguyennews/nguyennews/

For Love for You
National Archives file; *The Saskatoon Phoenix*; *The Secret Lives of Sgt. John Wilson: A True Story of Love & Murder* by Lois Simmie, Greystone Books, 2003; "Immigration Brought Crime" from Mahoney's Minute Men: The Saga of the Provincial Police 1917–1928 by Chris Stewart and Lynn Hudson, Modern Press, 1978

In His Mind
Court documents; reporter's notes; *Regina Leader-Post*.

It Would Explode the Heart
Court transcripts and documents; *Saskatoon StarPhoenix*; *The Globe and Mail*; Canadian Press; *Regina Leader-Post*.

The Darkness of the Night
National Archives file; *Manitoba Free Press*; *Moose Jaw Evening Times*.

Black and Blue
Court transcripts and documents; *Saskatoon StarPhoenix*.

No Place for Serenity
Saskatoon StarPhoenix; *Prince Albert Daily Herald*; *Regina Leader-Post*; *Edmonton Journal*.

Parlour Tricks
National Archives file; *Winnipeg Free Press*; *Regina Leader*; "Just like

the doctor ordered" by Myrna MacDonald from *Western People*, July 20, 1995; "Cold Blooded Murder" from *Mahoney's Minute Men: The Saga of the Provincial Police 1917–1928* by Chris Stewart and Lynn Hudson, 1978; "The Gervais Gang" from *Sheriffs and Outlaws* by Frank W. Anderson, Gopher Books.

Smoke and Mirrors
Regina Leader-Post; *The Globe and Mail*; *National Post*; CTV News, CBC Saskatchewan News, interviews; *From the Land of Shadows: The Making of Grey Owl* by Donald B. Smith, Western Producer Prairie Books, 1990; Websites: Charlie_smoke.tripod.com; www.legal affairs.org ("The strange tale of Charlie Smoke" by Michael Erard); wolf.resume.tripod.com.

The Mayor's Daughter
Court transcripts and documents; *Regina Leader-Post*; *Edmonton Journal*.

Unforgotten
Regina Leader-Post; court and police documents; reporter's notes; interviews with Marv Taylor.

The Painting
National Archives file; Regina Leader-Post; *Winnipeg Free Press*; "Killers on the Run" from *Western Canadian Desperadoes: Little Known Tales of the Old West* by Frank W. Anderson, Gopher Books.

Worlds Apart
Reporter's notes; court documents; *Regina Leader-Post*; *Saskatoon StarPhoenix*; National Parole Board decisions; Rockhampton *Morning Bulletin*; Website for the University of Melbourne.

About the Authors

Jana G. Pruden (right) is a graduate of the Nova Scotia College of Art and Design, and has a Bachelor of Fine Arts. She's been reporting on court and crime for the *Regina Leader-Post* since 2003, and is a columnist for the *Sun Community News*.

Born and raised in Regina, Barb Pacholik (left) is a graduate of the University of Regina's School of Journalism. Since 1988 she has worked as a reporter at the *Regina Leader-Post*, where most of her career has been spent covering crime and justice issues.

Dat